THE HEART OF THE FAITH

Basics of Christianity in Plain Language

Gary W. Demarest

WORD BOOKS
PUBLISHER
WACO, TEXAS

A DIVISION OF
WORD, INCORPORATED

Library of Congress Cataloging in Publication Data

Demarest, Gary W.
   The heart of the faith.

   1. Christian life—Presbyterian authors.
2. Theology, Doctrinal—Popular works. I. Title.
BV4501.2.D4419   1987   230   87-23029
ISBN 0-8499-3403-7 (pbk.)

Printed in the United States of America
7898 FG 987654321

*. . . from infancy you have
known the holy Scriptures,
which are able to make
you wise for salvation
through faith in Christ Jesus.*
2 Timothy 3:15

CONTENTS

INTRODUCTION

From time to time, someone asks me to recommend a book for a person who has little knowledge about the Christian faith and no background in Christian thought. For years, I've been recommending books by C. S. Lewis, J. B. Phillips, and Samuel Shoemaker.

But I'm increasingly aware that with the passage of time, there is always need for new expressions of the same old truths. I have no illusions that what I write will stand on a par with the writings of these giants. But I have felt these chapters on Christian basics "burning in my bones" to the point that I am being compelled to write.

I've tried to write from the perspective of the person on the street who expresses some interest in learning what we Christians are all about. And I've tried to avoid Christian jargon and clichés. In fact, I've done my best to reduce our Christian vocabulary to everyday language and thought.

These eight basics of Christian thought are not intended to be exhaustive. But I feel strongly that anyone exploring the meaning of Christian commitment can well begin with these concepts.

These chapters are not intended to be a substitute for regular and systematic Bible reading and study. I urge everyone exploring the Christian faith to get involved with a small group of believers who are committed to regular Bible study and to open sharing of their experiences with Christ.

Each of these chapters has grown out of personal encounters with explorers along the way. There is nothing I enjoy more than conversations with folks who come to me because they sincerely seek the meaning of Christ in their lives.

I have not written to prove or defend the faith. I write as a witness. I've never been driven by the need to win arguments or to convert people to my way of thinking or living. But since I began my journey with Jesus almost forty years ago, I've thoroughly enjoyed every opportunity to explain why I feel what I feel about Jesus and the life He gives to anyone who wants to listen.

If this book helps you in your exploration of what it means to be a Christian, I'll be grateful for the privilege of walking alongside you in what I consider to be the most exciting adventure the human spirit can know.

THE
HEART
OF
THE
FAITH

1

SIN

The recovery of a reasonable and workable view of sin is, perhaps, one of the most critical personal and social issues of our time. We best look for such a view somewhere between the harsh and inhumane approach of punishment of all sin as crime, and the extreme view of all sin as sickness needing only treatment.

A FIFTH-GRADE PUPIL in the Seattle schools penned the following answer on an anatomy exam: "The human body is composed of three parts: the Brainium, the Borax, and the Abominable Cavity. The Brainium contains the brain; the Borax contains the lungs, the liver, and the living things; and the Abominable Cavity contains the bowels, of which there are five—a, e, i, o, and u."

Our Seattle fifth-grader struggled with semantics. Obviously, the meaning of certain words had become greatly confused.

I think the same struggle is evident in much of our Christian vocabulary, especially with the word "sin." Here is a word that has suffered both from overuse and from neglect. Overuse in the sense that it is often used to describe nearly anything regarded as undesirable or unpleasant, and neglect in the sense that it has often been replaced with the concept of sickness.

In a series of lectures at Princeton Theological Seminary a few years ago, the eminent psychiatrist Dr. Karl Menninger raised the question with a gathering of clergy, "Whatever Became of Sin?" The lectures were later printed as a book with that title.

Menninger took the clergy to task for selling out to the therapeutic model of counseling that tries to solve most human problems without any specific reference to sin. In the book, Dr. Menninger traces the history by which we first moved from a concept of sin to crime and then to sickness.

In moving from sin to crime, Menninger deals with the period in American history when we began to legislate what were generally accepted Christian standards, requiring conformity and dealing with violations juridically. An example of this is the Sunday "blue" laws. Beginning with the commandment to keep the Sabbath holy, violations of Sabbath holiness are regarded as sins against God. When the Sabbath principle is made into civil law, banning, for example, commerce on Sundays, then violations become crimes, infractions of law. Laws were developed around most aspects of the moral code of the Bible, ranging from murder to adultery, with many things in between. Prohibition was an effort to deal with the problems relating to alcohol abuse from a legal standpoint, so that instead of dealing with drunkenness as sin, it was dealt with as crime.

Menninger argues further that it was only one more

step to move from dealing with sin as crime to dealing with sin as sickness. With the advent of psychotherapeutic views of human personality and behavior came the viewpoint that regards violations of the moral code as defects in the human psyche itself, thus some kind of sickness. Granted this basic viewpoint, the goal is to find both the causes and the cure of the sickness. Unfortunately, what may not be inevitable in this approach has become the norm in much psychiatric and psychotherapeutic practice. The individual is sometimes absolved from personal responsibility largely on the grounds that one cannot be held morally accountable for sickness. The development of this reasoning in the extreme is seen again and again in many legal defenses in the courtroom wherein the individual is absolved of responsibility for a crime due to mental or emotional sickness. The sickness, not the individual, is thus the cause of the crime; and treatment, not punishment, becomes the prescribed remedy.

I would hope that most of us would rather err on the side of mercy than on the side of judgment. I assume that we would prefer a judicial system more committed to the restoration and rehabilitation of criminals than to inhumane and violent punishment. But Menninger does well to raise the question, "Whatever became of sin?" He suggests that if there is to be any recovery in American thought of the biblical view of sin, it must come from the pulpits and pews of America's churches:

In all of the laments and reproaches made by our seers and prophets, one misses any mention of "sin" a word which used to be a veritable watchword of prophets. It was a word once in everyone's mind, but now rarely, if ever heard. Does that mean that no sin is involved in all of our troubles—sin with an "I" in the middle? Is no one any longer guilty of anything? Guilty perhaps of a sin that could be repented of and repaired and atoned for? Is it only that someone may be stupid or sick or criminal—or asleep? Wrong things are being done, we know; tares are being sown in the wheat field at night. But is no one responsible, no one answerable for these acts? Anxiety and depression we all acknowledge, and even vague guilt feelings; but has no one committed any sins? Where, indeed, did sin go? Whatever became of it?[1]

Perils and Pitfalls

The recovery of a reasonable and workable view of sin is, perhaps, one of the most critical personal and social issues of our time. We best look for such a view somewhere between the harsh and inhumane approach of punishment of all sin as crime, and the extreme view of all sin as sickness needing only treatment.

I find this workable view in the writings of the Bible. I must remind you of something that every serious student of Scripture knows: the Bible is neither a

1. Karl Menninger, *Whatever Became of Sin?* (New York: E. P. Dutton, 1973), 13.

textbook which systematically develops doctrines nor an encyclopedia in which we turn to "S" to find the doctrine of sin.

Because the Bible is a collection of writings centering in the experience of people over a long period of time, we discover variations in viewpoints about doctrinal matters that must be interpreted—and not always with mathematical certainty—within a particular context of time and place. This is especially true in examining the doctrine of sin. From the opening chapters of Genesis through the closing passages of Revelation, the concept of sin is present on virtually every page of the Bible.

Sin is introduced through human disobedience at the very beginning of human history. The root of sin is entangled in the exercise of human freedom in a way that either ignores or violates God's counsel and commands. Sin is only present when there has been some disclosure by God of what is expected or demanded. Sin is the refusal to give God his rightful due.

In pondering some of the biblical materials regarding sin, let me suggest two major pitfalls to be avoided, both amply illustrated in the long, difficult history of the doctrine of sin.

The Breaking of Rules

The first pitfall is that of regarding sin primarily as the breaking of rules. The shifting sands of moralism reveal the dangers of this approach. What is regarded as sinful in one culture may be quite desirable in another. What is labeled sinful at one point in time is later found to be acceptable.

Sin regarded primarily as the breaking of rules has a way of majoring upon minors. How well I remember my initial introduction to Christian legalism with regard to morals. When I first became a Christian, I was taught that smoking was a sin (and this admonition appeared long before there was any demonstrable connection between smoking and health). At the same time, I can't recall anyone suggesting that a day at the beach with one's girlfriend, which we young Californians took for granted, was contrary to Christian standards. Confusion entered on my first visit to a Christian Conference Center in Alabama in 1948, where many of the folks, including preachers, smoked with no sense of sin or guilt whatsoever. Yet what a shock to discover that men and women did not use the swimming pool at the same time. According to them, mixed (male and female) bathing was sinful!

Many years later, having lived and worked with different sizes and shapes of Christians in several countries and cultures, I'm aware that the accepted rules are as variable as cultures and climates. This is not to say standards are unimportant. But the fact is that such standards are best seen as rules by which a given group of people has chosen to live together without attempting to give them the force of divine law. I reject the idea that one's conduct must be consistent in every time and place. When I'm in East Africa, I try to observe the standards of the Christians in that culture, lest my actions get in the way of growing and caring relationships. But I make no pretense that I will maintain those same standards at home in La Canada.

I think the apostle Paul modeled this spiritual balance when he wrote to the Corinthians. There the issue was the burning question to them of whether or not one should eat meat that had first been offered to idols in a pagan temple and then later offered for sale (perhaps at a discount) in the local meat market. One group of Christians might argue that it was good stewardship to buy the meat at a lower price and give the margin to the poor. After all, we know idols have no real existence and the fact that the meat had been given in false worship had no particular consequence.

Another group of Christians, however, most likely recent converts from pagan religions, probably argued with passion that contact with anything remotely connected with their former way of worship had no place in their lives. For them, eating meat that had any possible connotation of pagan worship was indeed sinful.

Paul's summary in the midst of the irreconcilable Corinthian difference was:

> "Everything is permissible"—but not everything is beneficial. "Everything is permissible"—but not everything is constructive. Nobody should seek his own good, but the good of others.
>
> Eat anything sold in the meat market without raising questions of conscience, for, "The earth is the Lord's, and everything in it."

> If some unbeliever invites you to eat a meal and you want to go, eat whatever is put before you without raising questions of conscience. But if anyone says to you, "This has been offered in sacrifice," then do not eat it, both for the sake of the man who told you and for conscience' sake—the other man's conscience, I mean, not yours. For why should my freedom be judged by another's conscience? If I take part in the meal with thankfulness, why am I denounced because of something I thank God for?
>
> So whether you eat or drink or whatever you do, do it all for the glory of God. Do not cause anyone to stumble, whether Jews, Greeks or the church of God—even as I try to please everybody in every way. For I am not seeking my own good but the good of many, so that they may be saved. Follow my example, as I follow the example of Christ.
>
> (1 Cor. 10:23–31; 1 Cor. 11:1)

Every attempt to reduce Christian discipleship and behavior to a given set of rules inevitably becomes divisive or leads to triviality. Sin must be seen in the context of a personal relationship with God and others, not merely as a matter of adhering to rules and traditions.

Human Nature—Good or Evil

The second major pitfall to be avoided is regarding human nature as basically sinful and evil. The major emphasis of the opening chapters of Genesis is upon the goodness of God's creation: "And God saw that it was good . . . and God saw that it was good . . . and God saw that it was *very* good." Sin disrupts the goodness of God's creation. Men and women are not created as evil but as good. The fall is my story—the story of the misuse of God-given freedom. If I am created sinful, then I can hardly be held responsible for my sin. But if I am created in the moral and spiritual image of God with the capacity to do good, and if I choose to do evil, then surely I am responsible for my own sin.

The question might well be asked, "But what if I had never sinned?" I call it a theoretical question, because I've never met the person who could legitimately ask it! I insist that the Bible teaches that I have sinned—I have acted in willful disobedience to God's revealed counsel and commands—not because I had no choice in the matter by virtue of having a defective nature, but by my own choices for which I am responsible. I'm not sure whether or not I could have been perfect, but I surely could have done better than I have! I can't really blame Adam, Eve, *or* the snake!

To take my sin seriously, and to agree with Paul's statement that "all have sinned and fall short of the glory of God" (Rom. 3:23), is simply to state the obvious reality of botched-up freedom.

Sin Defined

It's hard for many of us moderns to take sin with the same seriousness as the Bible does. As Menninger pointed out, much contemporary preaching either avoids the subject entirely or develops elaborate explanations to relieve us from its seriousness.

But any reading, however casual, of the Scriptures demands the conclusion that the writers of the Bible, without exception, had a keen and compelling awareness of the pervasiveness, destructiveness, and tragedy of sin. Far from being difficult to find biblical passages referring to sin, it is difficult to find many chapters in the Bible which do not deal with sin or its consequences.

I know of no more comprehensive discussion of the many words and concepts used in the Bible to describe sin than the article entitled "Sin, Sinners," by S. J. De Vries in the *Interpreter's Dictionary of the Bible.* The article traces the usages of the many words employed for sin throughout the Old Testament, the Apocrypha and Pseudipigrapha, and the New Testament. De Vries begins by pointing out that some sense of estrangement between people and the Divine is basic to every religion. From the earliest times, the Hebrews demonstrated an awareness of sin as separation from God. The prophets warned of the tragic consequences that would follow the nation's disobedience to God, and the people learned it through experience. The New Testament regarded sin even more seriously, especially in the light of God's costly and gracious way of dealing with it—Christ's death and resurrection.

The most common words for sin in the Old and New Testaments are also the least theological, in the sense that their root idea is that of *missing the mark* or *taking the wrong road.* Clearly that is one of the basic and essential concepts in our understanding of sin. Here the emphasis is upon error, wrong choice, failure, intellectual error, or moral fault. Many words are used for sin in the general sense of sin as *disobedience, transgressions of laws, wickedness,* or *evil actions.*

Although they are not used as extensively, the words with the most profound meaning of sin in relationship to God are those generally translated in English as *ungodliness* and *unrighteousness.* Here is sin in the sense of our refusal to worship God as God, our refusal to seek the glory and the righteousness of God in all our relationships and actions. Brokenness in relationships, disintegration of personality, destructive behaviors—all are products of our refusal to seek and worship God in spirit and in truth.

There are times when Paul, especially, speaks of sin as an independent force, a power outside of and hostile to us. Sin is then our capitulation to that power in which we become captive to the forces of evil.

The religious people of Jesus' day, such as the Pharisees, had no difficulty viewing the "godless" Gentiles as sinners on all counts. The conflict came when Jesus taught that *all* men and women, good and bad, religious and irreligious, believers and unbelievers, were sinners and rightly under God's judgment.

Always in the Bible, any discovery or experience of life as God intended it to be begins with the recognition

and acceptance of our personal estrangement from God.
We recognize this separation as the result of personal
sin—sin for which we are individually accountable to
God. While ignorance is sometimes regarded as a partial
justification, no one is ever excused of personal responsibility to God—nor is anyone ever considered beyond
saving.

The Remedy for Sin

If anything, the New Testament takes a more stern
view of sin than the Old Testament does. While the New
Testament is relentless in its warnings against the tragic
consequences of sin, it admonishes in order to convince
us that we need God's remedy for that sin.

Doesn't the human body sometimes work the same
way? From time to time, my body develops some pain
or other symptom that keeps demanding my attention.
How grateful I have become for competent physicians
who can give me a proper diagnosis—and I become even
more grateful when I learn that there is a remedy for my
need.

To me, there are four basic and essential steps we
must take in order to experience God's remedy for our sin.

Awareness

The first step is recognizing the problem. The Bible
tells the story of many men and women, whose journey to

wholeness out of brokenness began with the moment of recognition of their sin. David, in Psalm 51, for instance, cried out, "Against thee, and thee only, have I sinned!" To see our sins as offenses, not only against others or ourselves, but against God, is the only beginning point for experiencing God's remedy for sin.

The refusal to worship God as God lies at the root of all brokenness and hurt in human relationships. The greatest tragedy of all is our refusal to recognize the source of our brokenness. How often do we simply make the wrong diagnosis of our ills because we don't really take God into account? By this, I don't intend to imply that all problems can be solved and all relationships healed by saying a prayer. But I find no encouragement in the Bible for any remedy for sin and its tragic consequences apart from an initial recognition that we are accountable to God for our attitudes, behaviors, and actions.

Confession

While recognition of one's sin is vital, it is not the whole solution to the problem. The second aspect of God's remedy calls us to *confession*. A literal translation of the basic New Testament word translated as "confession" is "to agree with." Confession involves an open agreement with God as to the seriousness of personal sin. Again, in Psalm 51, we hear David's confession to God, the open admission to God of wrongdoing.

Sometimes our confession to God needs to be accompanied by confession to another person. Like so many other good decisions, however, this practice is not without potential peril. An intriguing passage in James admonishes us to confess our sins to each other. The context of the passage is too often ignored, for confession to each other is called for as a part of the healing ministry of the Christian community. The passage needs to be read in its entirety:

> Is any one of you in trouble? He should pray. Is anyone happy? Let him sing songs of praise. Is any one of you sick? He should call the elders of the church to pray over him and anoint him with oil in the name of the Lord. And the prayer offered in faith will make the sick person well; the Lord will raise him up. If he has sinned, he will be forgiven. Therefore confess your sins to each other and pray for each other so that you may be healed. The prayer of a righteous man is powerful and effective.
> (James 5:13–16)

The obvious conclusion from this passage is that there are occasions when sickness is a result of sin. But this is also a way of making it clear that not all sickness is a result of sin. But when the sickness is a product of sin, the clear teaching is that confession to each other is an inherent part of the prayer for healing.

In pastoral practice, I have seen many horror stories of inappropriate confession. For this reason, we must not take this admonition lightly. Certainly not all sins should be confessed to others. Too often, confession is used to clear one's conscience without regard to the devastating effects that the confession may have upon the other person.

Some people have greater need than others to confess certain sins to another person. While this can be of great value, and sometimes essential, it must also be recognized as having great potential for widespread hurt and pain. A context of inviolable confidentiality and trust is absolutely essential.

All sins must be confessed to God, but caution must be exercised in the confession to others. There's a lot of merit in the Roman Catholic tradition of confessing to a priest in absolute confidentiality, when that confession to another person, as well as to God, enables the person to leave the matter there without bringing hurt and pain to others.

Repentance

Confession without repentance can become a sham and a travesty. And repentance must not be confused with merely being sorry. We can be very sorry for sin—especially when we've been found out—without actually ever repenting. Repentance in the Bible has to do with *actions,* not merely *feelings.* Repentance is best described as an act in which we turn around and go in another direction; repentance is intentionally moving out on another road.

You may recall that one of the root ideas for sin is that of taking the wrong road. Repentance means that I seek to go back to the point of wrong departure and get on the right road.

This decision to turn and walk a different way becomes the crucial point, for instance, in the rehabilitation of the person with an alcohol or drug problem. How many people have come to me with these problems, genuinely smitten with sorrow for their miserable patterns of behavior. But without the kind of repentance grounded in a commitment to move out on a different road in the context of a caring and supporting community, the devastating patterns of abuse tend to continue.

Forgiveness

The final step of God's remedy is forgiveness realized. I add the word *realized* to forgiveness because forgiveness has no meaning apart from its realization. The offer of God's forgiveness in and through Christ has no strings attached. But until I can accept it as a working reality in my life, nothing has really happened.

This pivotal point of forgiveness is where I have found the power of the Christian community at its best. Again and again, I have received the assurance of forgiveness through another person or in a small group. This acceptance thus becomes a strong, constant reminder of God's forgiveness. When I realize forgiveness from another person, I am more keenly aware of forgiveness by God.

Forgiveness need not be equated with forgetting. I disagree strongly with those who insist that forgiveness always means forgetting. There are some sins that I will never be able to forget. In fact, their memory might be a positive factor in my not repeating them. But forgiveness enables me to live with the memory of past sins and failures, and at the same time, celebrate the reality of forgiveness. Forgiveness takes away the power from the memory of past sin.

Whatever else is certain in life, I will never escape the reality of continuing sin—in thought, in deed, and in word. But what is also as certain is the good news that God is ever reaching out to me with his forgiveness. Realizing the consistency of God's mercy, forgiveness gives me the strength and hope to live in the climate of Christ's prayer: "Forgive us our sins, as we forgive those who sin against us."

2

SALVATION

. . . *salvation is the central theme of the entire Bible. Of all the things we might say about Christianity, we must say that it is a religion of salvation. Old Testament scholars have long pointed out that "God" and "Savior" are synonymous throughout the Old Testament. The God of the Bible is the God who, from the very beginning of human history, has been about the process of saving people from the consequences of their own disobedience and sinfulness.*

THE TOUR OF WESTMINSTER ABBEY had been impressive indeed, especially to the woman from Kansas on this her first trip ever to Great Britain. As she viewed the burial places of eminent leaders of the past and listened to the eloquent tour guide describe the glories of British history enshrined within the renowned Abbey she was overjoyed to be in this Christian shrine.

The guide gathered his little group one last time in the rear of the awesome Nave and asked for any final questions before dismissing the group. Without hesitation, she raised her hand. "Yes, madam, what is your question?" asked the guide. "Just tell me one thing, young man. Has anyone been *saved* here lately?"

Needless to say, the guide was nonplussed and the group was amused at her quaint query. Even in one of the best-known churches of Christendom, salvation language had come on hard times.

If you're like me, someone initiating a conversation with "Brother, are you saved?" isn't likely to get your undivided attention or warmest response. As a matter of fact, I will probably try to duck out of the conversation as quickly as possible.

Admitting my aversion to this salvation vernacular, I still must face up to the fact that salvation is the central theme of the entire Bible. Of all the things we might say about Christianity, we must say that it is a religion of salvation. Old Testament scholars have long pointed out that "God" and "Savior" are synonymous throughout the Old Testament. The God of the Bible is the God who, from the very beginning of human history, has been about the process of saving people from the consequences of their own disobedience and sinfulness.

The very name *Jesus,* from the Old Testament *Joshua,* literally means "God the Savior" or "God is salvation." Six times in the letters to Timothy and Titus, Jesus is called "God our Savior." The full title given to Him in all Christian tradition is "Our Lord and Savior, Jesus Christ."

The idea of salvation is absolutely essential to any understanding of the Scriptures of the Old and New Testaments. And yet salvation language can be embarrassing, repugnant, or downright amusing to all too many moderns, both within and without the Christian community.

To communicate the meaning of salvation with clarity and emphasis in today's world, Christians must bring some new language to bear upon this great central theme of our faith.

But "bringing in some new language" is not without peril. For the danger comes when we make salvation into something other than what it really is in the Bible. A fresh translation or interpretation is one thing, but a changing of the original meaning is something else. And too often, in the name of doing the former, theology actually results in the latter.

On Being Lost

A good place to begin is by developing a clear understanding of why the Bible takes salvation so seriously. People need to be saved because they are lost.

During my college and seminary years, one of my summer jobs was lifeguarding at a Southern California beach. One of the first things we learned in our final training was to expect resistance from most victims who are being rescued. I had serious doubts about that part of my training. It seemed to me that anyone needing help in a riptide or undertow, or anyone being battered by surf beyond his ability to control, would eagerly welcome assistance or outright rescue. But experience quickly verified my trainer's instruction. I had a fight on my hands from virtually every person being assisted or rescued, probably at least seventy-five percent of the time, from women and men alike.

More than a few of us don't like to admit that we

need help. And I'm one of them! Just ask my wife; she'll tell you that a recent experience in London was typical. For two weeks, we had been completely on our own in a rental car. We had begun from Heathrow Airport, driven west through Cornwall, up through King Arthur country and on through Wales, enjoying the entire coastal, scenic route. Then we moved through the Lake Country into Scotland, all the way to John-o-Groat at the northern tip of the Highlands. Then, returning south through Edinburgh and York, we made our last stop at Canterbury Cathedral.

We had driven almost three thousand miles (on a six-hundred-mile island) without a hitch. After a leisurely supper in a delightful little restaurant in Canterbury, I asked the owner for his advice on the best route to Heathrow, where we were to spend our final night before flying home to Los Angeles. He aimed me on a direct route to Heathrow that was to take us through the southern part of London. We arrived in the greater London area just as it was getting dark, and somewhere I had obviously missed a turn or two. With map in hand and navigator in passenger's seat, I was quite certain we could work our way through town to the airport.

Our marriage underwent severe strain as Marily kept insisting with great urgency that I stop and ask directions. It was with more than a little reluctance that I finally surrendered to her pleading. Even then, I managed to get lost again, demonstrating my competence by ending up crossing the Vauxhall Bridge right into Victoria

Station in the midst of the post-theater traffic jams in the center of London. At least I was proud that I knew where I was, even though I didn't know how to get where I was trying to go. Needless to admit, our scheduled early evening arrival at the Sheraton Heathrow didn't happen until early morning!

Whether drowning in the ocean or wandering around London, there's something inside us that fiercely resists admitting we're lost and asking to be saved.

One of the things most easily overlooked is the fact that when we are most in need of saving is often the time when we most vehemently deny our predicament. This is a well-established fact known by every recovering alcoholic. The first step to sobriety is the open and honest admission of one's problem with alcohol, along with the acceptance of the fact that outside help is needed, both from the "higher power" and from others alongside.

On Being Saved

Driving through central California late one night, I was pushing the buttons on my car radio, hoping for some interesting company to keep me awake. I heard an offer being made by a religious broadcaster: "Send for our free pamphlet on 'How to Get Your Lost Loved Ones Saved.'" Instinctively, my mind reacted in negative protest.

I'm convinced that one of the basic reasons for the sad plight of salvation language in our time is this idea that salvation is something we can make happen to other people. Not only does this assumption cut across the grain of human nature, but it reflects a misunderstanding of the Bible's teaching about salvation.

If I were unfortunate enough to be the "unsaved loved one" of the person informed by the "how to" approach of getting others saved, I would most likely have my defenses up against all efforts to coerce or manipulate me into something I wasn't convinced I needed in the first place.

Salvation, according to Scripture, is exclusively something that God does for a person. That is precisely the issue of salvation—it isn't something that I can do for myself, and it is nothing that anyone other than God can do for me.

Again let me draw from the wisdom of Alcoholics Anonymous. Sobriety is not something that you can bring to the alcoholic; the person with the drinking problem can't be coerced or manipulated into sobriety. You won't find a booklet in the AA library describing "How to Get Your Loved Ones Sober." You will be told, however, that only the person with the problem can decide whether or not to seek sobriety.

In the same way, we must get beyond the notion that salvation is something we can bring to someone else, or even to ourselves. Salvation is the work of God the Savior. It can be received only as a gift from Him.

The best way we can be of help to others is by making the way of salvation clear to them. And we really don't have to use theological language to do it. It comes off quite clearly when seen in two directions. Salvation means that we are saved *from* . . . and *for* . . . .

Saved From . . .

Perhaps the most common use of salvation language today relates to the concept of salvation as *wholeness,* one of the root ideas of the words used for salvation in Scripture. This idea of wholeness is readily recognized against the backdrop of the brokenness all around us.

Salvation can certainly be presented as a deliverance from the tyranny of the false gods and saviors found at the root of much of our brokenness today. The god of science and technology, for example, is certainly hallowed by many intelligent people. Science and technology are incredibly useful and helpful, of course. I certainly don't want to go back to "the good old days" prior to radio, television, jet travel, computers, space exploration, improved health, and longevity through modern medicine.

But technological breakthroughs have not given us ultimate clues to our sense of meaning. Nor are we doing all that well in human relationships. It's now painfully clear that our technology may create the very monsters by which we will destroy ourselves unless we can control them by a greater power. Without some giant strides in the control of military armaments—nuclear, chemical, and conventional—the future is undeniably frightening and bleak. Even to believe that mere superiority in technological strength and weaponry can "save" us begs the point of what substance actually constitutes salvation.

Salvation appeals to me as deliverance from false faith in science and technology. Not from *all* faith, mind you, for there are many products of technology which merit a high level of trust. Every time I fasten my seat belt for my flight to San Francisco, I place a high level of faith in technology. When I take prescribed medication or undergo surgery, I am trusting medical science. But this kind of trust, superior as it has become, is nevertheless limited. Salvation frees me from placing ultimate trust for my eternal wellbeing in science and technology.

Science and technology aren't the only modern gods vying for our commitment. Another god ever active and demanding is the state. Governments demand a great deal of faith. Whether it's called patriotism or nationalism, the net result tends to be the same—demands for absolute loyalty. And when you're a citizen of a government grounded in democratic principles, with the right of people's choices a basic tenet, there can be a subtle temptation to confuse the state with the Kingdom of God.

I'm convinced that the crucial political issue to be resolved by American Christians in the closing decade of the twentieth century lies right here. And it's just as much an issue for those on the left as for those on the right of the political spectrum. I work within a denomination, for instance, in which the prevailing political and social views expressed are termed liberal. But now, coming on as a much stronger force is the evangelical right that consistently nudges us on from the ultraconservative side of the scene.

To me, the primary issue is not who will win the battles concerning the issues of abortion, prayer in schools, pornography, military budgets, and social welfare programs. The ultimate danger on both sides is the failure to make a sharp distinction between any and all philosophies of government and the Kingdom of God.

If we equate American democracy with the Kingdom of God in any way, we have fallen into the trap of idolizing the state. If we tie the future of the Christian church to any particular government, we have entered the arena of idolatry. And anyone with even a cursory knowledge of Israel's history in the Old Testament and of the beginning church in the New, knows what God thinks of idolatry.

A phrase that has a long, bloody history in human affairs is "God and country." A certain theologian I admire warns against placing anything alongside of God, suggesting that the formula "God and *anything*" always results in idolatry!

As an American, I'm grateful to have been born as a citizen within this great heritage. I'm committed to responsible citizenship—that's why I served two terms on our local school board as well as on several other governmental committees and commissions at the local and state levels. That's why I take voting and communicating with our elected representatives seriously. But I stubbornly refuse to expect from the state what I can expect only from the Kingdom of God.

Salvation frees us *from* the false worship of the state. Jesus and Paul made the distinction quite clearly, and we do well to follow their admonitions. We must take citizenship seriously, aware that we are among the most fortunate Christians in the world to live without fear of persecution in the normal exercise of our faith. But *never* can we afford to equate the state with the Kingdom of God.

No discussion of contemporary gods can be complete, for they are myriad in number and in their sphere of influence. Certainly the god of materialism, in the guise not only of affluence but of financial security as well, should be unmasked daily by those who are prone to translate affluence into a sign of God's blessing. If such were the case, God must take a dim view of at least seventy-five percent of the people presently living on our little planet.

And then there's the god of unrestrained sexual freedom who's really on a roll right now, at least in the West. In a game of Trivial Pursuit with our family the other evening, one question asked, "What was the price of the first issue of *Playboy* magazine?" Our teenagers were surprised, first, that I knew the answer (fifty cents), but even more that I was an adult when *Playboy* began (about 1952). I was reminded of the incredible changes that have taken place in our part of the world in public attitudes toward sexuality and sexual behavior in the course of my adult life.

How we can work our way out of the situation we're in is a source of concern. How we're going to control pornography, much less define it, will be the scene of many battles in the future. But an even greater concern is what happens to folks, especially in their formative years, who somehow believe that unrestrained sexual pleasure can provide a rich and satisfying life. The shipwrecks of precious people, both young and old, who have drifted into this storm of deceit are scattered all over.

Salvation as the freedom *from* the incessant, destructive demands of sexual drives is a welcome liberation. But this salvation doesn't mean rejection of all that is beautiful and fun in God's delightful creation of males and females. Salvation from the false worship of the god of romping sexuality offers the possibility of discovering how exciting *good sex* can really be!

If you have even a casual knowledge of the Bible, you're aware that we still haven't touched on the most prevalent meaning of salvation taught in the Scriptures. And that is salvation from the standpoint of the remedy of our separation and alienation from God as the wages of sin. Any view of salvation not anchored in the need to be reconciled to God fails to be faithful to the central message of the Scriptures.

This is where many contemporary interpretations of salvation are seriously lacking. If salvation is seen primarily as a matter of physical, psychological, or emotional wholeness, there is a real danger that the gospel might be missed. To be sure, personal wholeness is a normal product of salvation. But until we have squarely faced and fully dealt with the problem of our need to be reunited with God, we have not even begun to deal with the question of salvation.

It is true that salvation gives us the insight, perspective, and power to expose and reject false gods. But other approaches to developing an understanding of the problem of evil can afford dangerously deceptive "solutions" as well. For example, many folks overcome the power of materialism, unbridled sex, or destructive nationalism without inviting our Lord and Savior Jesus Christ into the picture. But until they have genuinely confronted their primary need—reconciliation with God—they still haven't touched the biblical concept of salvation in its essence.

Recently I had a stimulating conversation with a well-known person in public life. He shared the fact that he had quit drinking more than ten years ago. He then went on to share that he had never been involved in Alcoholics Anonymous, nor was the Christian faith or church important to him. When his physician advised him to quit drinking because of a diagnosed liver ailment, he simply quit drinking. He's an exception to the vast number of people with an alcohol problem, and we can't deny that he's been "saved" from his problem. But he professes no relationship to salvation in the biblical sense.

Saved For . . .

The best way to avoid the malady of missing God is to keep the second dimension of salvation as closely tied to the first as heads and tails on a coin. Salvation *from* is also salvation *for*.

We can deal with numerous aspects of freedom *from* the power of the false gods and experience certain areas of wholeness, but biblical salvation always focuses upon the positive results of salvation with regard to God, to oneself, and to the community of believers.

Salvation is a gift of God in which He creates us anew for a relationship with Himself. In the deepest sense, it is a spiritual mystery which does not lend itself to critical analysis. That's why I said at the outset that salvation is not something we can do for ourselves or for others.

Just as God created us for Himself, so a new creation by God is enacted in salvation. The sinful individual, alienated from God, is re-created by a sovereign act of the Almighty, and reconciliation is that new reality. The power for this restoration resides only in God, and the good news is that He has initiated that reconciliation in His Son, Jesus Christ.

In that reconciliation with God, we are saved *for* participation in the new community of God's people. In this sense, salvation, though personal, is never a private matter. When salvation neglects our incorporation into the body of Christ, it is not biblical salvation. There is no such thing as an exclusive relationship with God. As salvation brings reconciliation with God, it also brings reconciliation with the people of God in the creation of a fellowship of men and women bound together in Christ's holy love.

In the context of the new relationship with God and with His people, there flows the potential *for* wholeness. One is set free from the bondage of death and decay, truly free to live *for* God within the new community of His people toward personal wholeness in every area of life.

Even death itself doesn't mark the end of the journey. We are being saved *for* eternal life, with strong confidence in the One who died and rose from the dead.

In a recent interview on American television, Bishop Desmond Tutu of South Africa was questioned by ABC's Ted Koppel. Discussing the possibility of expanding bloodshed and violence in South Africa, Koppel asked Tutu: "Aren't you discouraged and pessimistic about the future?" Replied Tutu: "Yes, humanly speaking. I am very discouraged and terribly frightened about what may happen to thousands of my people. But, for those of us who are shaped by the life, death, and resurrection of Jesus Christ, we face the uncertain future with hope and love, knowing that nothing in heaven or on earth can separate us from God's love in Christ."

That's what salvation is all about!

3

BORN AGAIN

There are numerous vital signs of spiritual life, but perhaps the most basic is an awareness of God that centers in Jesus Christ. One who has been born again becomes consciously aware of the love and the presence of God and, most likely, develops some practices through prayer and Bible reading to enhance and expand that awareness into all the activities and seasons of life.

I WAS BROWSING in the religion section of my favorite bookstore. "You're interested in religion?" a young man asked. Nodding, I sensed that he was almost ready to pounce. "How interested are you?" he continued. It was quite obvious that he intended to pursue his line of thought no matter what my reply. It wasn't long before the key question came: "Are you born again?" My answer, of course, was affirmative.

"*When* were you born again?" I proceeded to share with him my testimony. His restlessness indicated he didn't really want to hear my story, and he interrupted, "But *when* were you born again?" It was clear to me by now that we weren't on the same wavelength. For my commitment to Christ had come over a long period of time and actually came into focus through a Bible study group on the campus at Cal Berkeley during my senior year.

"But you haven't answered my question. *When* were you born again?" Now I *knew* that we weren't speaking the same language. I excused myself, sorry indeed that we weren't communicating as brothers in Christ.

This scene in the bookstore reveals a widespread misunderstanding throughout the Christian community. And all because of broken communication. On another occasion, a troubled parishioner came into my study, deeply upset because her teenage son had become a "born-again" Christian. "You certainly don't believe in this 'born-again' Christianity!" she said. To me, she was caught in the same error as the young man in the bookstore.

Any idea that "born again" refers to some particular type of conversion experience or to some species of Christian persons is contrary to what is taught in the Bible.

Jesus and Nicodemus

Any discussion of "born again" must focus upon John 3:1–18. Here is the memorable story of the conversation of Nicodemus with Jesus:

> Now there was a man of the Pharisees named Nicodemus, a member of the Jewish ruling council. He came to Jesus at night and said, "Rabbi, we know you are a teacher who has come from God. For no one could perform the miraculous signs you are doing if God were not with him."
> In reply Jesus declared, "I tell you the truth,

unless a man is born again, he cannot see the kingdom of God."

"How can a man be born when he is old?" Nicodemus asked. "Surely he cannot enter a second time into his mother's womb to be born!"

Jesus answered, "I tell you the truth, unless a man is born of water and the Spirit, he cannot enter the kingdom of God. Flesh gives birth to flesh, but the Spirit gives birth to spirit. You should not be surprised at my saying, 'You must be born again.' The wind blows wherever it pleases. You hear its sound, but you cannot tell where it comes from or where it is going. So it is with everyone born of the Spirit."

"How can this be?" Nicodemus asked.

"You are Israel's teacher," said Jesus, "and do you not understand these things? I tell you the truth, we speak of what we know, and we testify to what we have seen, but still you people do not accept our testimony. I have spoken to you of earthly things and you do not believe; how then will you believe if I speak of heavenly things? No one has ever gone into heaven except the one who came from heaven—the Son of Man. Just as Moses lifted up the snake in the desert, so the Son of Man must be lifted up, that everyone who believes in him may have eternal life."   (John 3:1–15)

Lest we mold the phrase "born again" into an unbreakable cliché, we must remember that it occurs only this one time in the gospels. In New Testament language, it is the word *anothen* and can be translated either "born again," "born from above," or "born anew." The fact that this expression is used only once by John should keep us from making it into an overworked generic term describing some special kind of Christian.

When someone asks me if I'm a "born-again" Christian, I want to reply, "What other kind is there?" I'm quite certain that's what Nicodemus would say.

It had been an unforgettable night for Nicodemus. Like almost everyone else in Jerusalem, this man realized that his curiosity had been captured by the reports about the mysterious rabbi from Galilee, Jesus of Nazareth. Unlike other rabbis, this Jesus "taught with authority" (Matt. 7:29). His teaching had a ring of truth about it. In addition, His words were accompanied by many "mighty works" such as cleansing lepers and healing people born blind. There were even some reports that He had exercised special powers over nature itself.

These reports were of special interest to Nicodemus since he was a member of the Sanhedrin, the council of seventy men who were responsible for maintaining the doctrines and traditions of Jewish faith and practice. As a Pharisee, Nicodemus was among the most orthodox of all, strictly holding each of the 438 regulations that had been developed from the law given to Moses at Mt. Horeb.

Nicodemus was an honorable man. He would not come to conclusions about Jesus without firsthand experience. He could have come to Jesus at night for various reasons. Since Jesus was increasingly being sought out by large crowds, Nicodemus may have made arrangements to see Him when he could be assured of being alone and unhurried. Or perhaps Nicodemus thought it best to meet secretly to avoid undue speculation and potential controversy. Apparently some members of the Sanhedrin would have considered it a traitorous act just to spend time privately with this upstart rabbi. Or perhaps the "after-hours" meeting was suggested by Jesus out of His desire for quality time with Nicodemus without interruption.

I find myself liking Nicodemus from the very start. He breaks the stereotype of the Scribes and Pharisees. He doesn't bristle with hostility nor does he argue to prove Jesus wrong. His opening words, "Good teacher," denote genuine respect, not derision. He affirms the mighty works that Jesus has done. Unlike those who had attributed Christ's works to the devil, Nicodemus recognized them as signs of God's presence and power. As a man steeped in the Scriptures, Nicodemus certainly knew that such signs must accompany the coming of the Messiah. I assume that Nicodemus was at least open to the possibility that Jesus might indeed be the One whom Israel had hoped for so long.

The story of Nicodemus gives hope to all who will come to Jesus with openness. The early years of my ministry were spent working with high school and college youth. Typically, they wanted coherent demonstration and positive proof in order to make a commitment to Jesus as Savior and Lord. I remember one student in particular—Larry Svane, a varsity swimmer at the University of Washington. We had started a Bible study group in the Beta House, and Larry came out of sheer curiosity at the invitation of his roommate. From the outset, it was clear that Larry had deep intellectual difficulties with nearly everything relating to the idea of God. In our journey through the Gospel of Mark, I urged him to make two lists, one of those things which he could affirm, and a second of those things which he could not accept or understand.

I learned from Larry that there is a vast difference between a skeptic and a struggler. At first, he believed very little about God and Jesus. But he was always open to new ideas. He was always willing to consider the possibility that there just might be ultimate truth in this Man Jesus. At first, Larry's list of doubts far outweighed his record of affirmations. But as time went by, more and more items disappeared from the second list and appeared on the first. Larry approached Jesus with an openness that was refreshing. And I've long since come to believe that our Lord honors and respects that kind of openness. I can't say that everyone who uses this approach will come to faith in Christ, but I can tell you that Larry did. This young man who was such a sincere struggler spiritually is now a minister of the gospel in Pittsburgh.

Little did Nicodemus expect to hear what Jesus said, nor could he grasp what the Rabbi meant. I've always felt that Nicodemus had a hard time understanding the idea of being "born again," not because he was bad but because he was so good. Nicodemus was not unlike the rich young ruler in that he had kept the Law with utmost perseverance. He was a devout man, one who could be trusted. If he had been a scoundrel or a crook, then the idea of a new birth might have made more sense to him. Obviously, immoral people need to be born all over again—they need a new beginning in order to live by a higher standard.

For Nicodemus, the idea of a new birth must have seemed preposterous at first. After all, he hadn't done all that poorly with his first birth. Did he not trust the living God? Wasn't he a man of prayer and devotion? Weren't justice and righteousness basic to his daily life? Couldn't he say with the rich young ruler, "All these things I have kept from my youth"?

Perhaps Nicodemus's reply questioning the possibility of re-entry into his mother's womb is best understood as Middle East humor in which gross exaggeration produces a good belly laugh. Nicodemus was too much the scholar and clear thinker to ask this question literally. He knew, as well as we do, that there is no way physically to be born again. Why, then, the question? With a bit of daring, to draw Jesus out a little more, I think the question had the intent of asking for added light on this intriguing idea.

Have you ever wished you could start all over again? I have. I certainly don't claim to have been as good as Nicodemus, but I've never been a bad person in terms of ethics and morals. Even so, I've had plenty of reasons to wish I could erase the slate clean. This idea wasn't at all foreign to the people of Israel. There was a marvelous moment on the Day of Atonement each year when a ceremonial act granted everyone a new beginning. In that action, the priest laid his hands on a goat before sending it outside the camp never to return. With the departure of the goat, the priest promised the people that their sins were being carried out into the wilderness to be remembered no more. In Israelite culture, there was another occasion of new beginnings. After a sabbath of sabbath years, seven times seven, the Year of Jubilee was celebrated. Every fifty years, all property returned to its original owners and all debts were forgiven. It was a glorious time of new beginning!

The idea of Jesus as "the Lamb of God who takes away the sin of the world" is basic to the idea of being born again. In declaring the possibility of being born again, Jesus is offering Nicodemus another beginning, an entirely new way of experiencing life.

Life in the Spirit

It's not even debatable that one must be physically born to experience physical life. There's no shortage of lively, often heated debate these days as to when the life of a person truly begins. I'll never forget my feelings when I saw the ultra-sound pictures of our daughter's first child taken during the twentieth week of pregnancy. To see the head, the arms, and the legs; and to hear the little heart beating rapidly, brought an overwhelming sense of mystery and wonder. There was no question in my mind that a life had already begun and that a person was being formed moment by moment. As of this writing, the baby has not yet been born, and until there is a physical birthing, that child will not know physical life as we have come to know it.

The logic of the gospel is based on the premise that there are two kinds of life, physical and spiritual. There is a life of the body, and there is a life of the spirit. As the life of the body requires a physical birth, so the life of the spirit requires a spiritual birth. This is the basic reality which Jesus brought to Nicodemus.

The language of the New Testament is more precise at this point than English. Our word "life" is used to translate two different words, *bios* and *zoay*. *Bios* is always used to refer to physical life, the life of the body. *Zoay* is always used to refer to the life of the spirit. In New Testament thought, it's possible to have *bios* without having *zoay*. In other words, one can be physically alive but spiritually dead.

From time to time, folks ask me whether or not I believe that all persons are children of God. I don't hesitate to answer this one with a *yes* and a *no*. Certainly *yes* in the sense of "bios," in that every person on this planet shares all the realities of physical life in common. In that sense, I have no hesitancy in affirming that every human being is a child of God. But when it comes to "zoay," I have to say *no* or disagree with Jesus. Life in the spirit transcends physical life. It is more than mere biological existence. There is all the difference in the world between physical existence and spiritual life. This life of the spirit has to do with caring, loving, and feeling in the light of God's loving, active presence.

It was this aspect of life that Jesus taught, lived, and produced. This was what Jesus meant when He said, "I have come that they might have life, and have it to the full" (John 10:10). This is what John affirms: "He who has the Son has life; he who does not have the Son of God does not have life" (1 John 5:12).

In a marvelous passage, C. S. Lewis observes that a person who changes from having "bios" to having "zoay" experiences as big a change as a statue which changes from being a carved stone to being a real man. And that is precisely what Christianity is all about. The world is a great sculptor's shop; we are the statues. And there is a rumor going around the shop that some of us will come to life one day.

How to Be Born Again

The turning point in the conversation between Nicodemus and Jesus came with the question, "How can this be?" The great moment came when Nicodemus moved beyond intellectual sparring to personal quest. This is always the case. Whenever I'm involved in Christ and Christian commitment, I pray and listen carefully for this moment. It doesn't always come. Sometimes the person never gets beyond apparent intellectual curiosity or argumentative debate. And there's not much point inviting someone to receive a gift when that person only wants to argue whether such a gift even exists, is there?

But what a delightful moment to witness the opening up of a person's life to the new birth! This is what I call the "How can this be?" moment. Too often we're prone to miss the moment, continuing to guide an individual's intellectual climb when he really wants to be still and seek the personal.

I'll never forget such a conversation with a bright collegian. During our fifth or sixth session together, he had no shortage of tough questions about Christ. But he brought me up short in that conversation, blurting out, "Could you just put away your theology and tell me *how* I can experience Christ?" Obviously I had missed the "How can this be?" moment.

What did Jesus say to Nicodemus in that moment? He moved directly to a gracious offer! Immediately He focused on what had not yet happened, His death on the cross. We must never minimize the centrality of Christ's death to the new birth. He was lifted up on the cross "that everyone who believes in him may have eternal life" (John 3:15).

There's a trend today to offer new life in Christ with little or no reference to the meaning of His death on the cross. We invite people to come to Christ in order to satisfy their need for meaning, to resolve some particular crisis, or even to experience the warmth of a caring community. Certainly these are all important benefits, advantages which usually gain a positive response. But products of Christian conversion cannot preclude the centrality of forgiveness.

The essence of the Gospel is God's offer of forgiveness and eternal life. This forgiveness is inseparably linked to Christ's death on the cross. I don't pretend to understand fully *how* Christ's death accomplishes the forgiveness of my sins, but I can't escape the fact that this is the nucleus of the gospel. Only when I recognize my need for forgiveness can I be born again.

The danger at this early point of our search is that we fall into the trap of developing formulas and techniques to bring people into the new birth. Billy Graham tells the story of the beleaguered inquirer who had come forward in response to the appeal of an evangelist to accept Christ and be born again. The first person he met slapped him on the back and said, "Hold on!" The next person put his arms around his shoulder and said, "Let go!" And someone else shouted, "Just praise the Lord!" Needless to say, the result was one confused questioner.

If we view spiritual life as somewhat analogous to physical life, we begin by affirming the fact that a birth is essential. Could we not also say that consciousness of that birth is all-important? I have no doubt whatever that I have been born physically. How do I know? To be sure, through the years my parents have talked to me about various aspects of my birth. And I do have a birth certificate which attests to that event. Not long ago I met a man in Uganda who had never known his parents. His father had died before he was born and his mother died shortly after. Thus he had no birth certificate—in fact, there were none in his tribal village. Does his lack of evidence mean that he was any less born than I was? Of course not!

The evidence of birth is life. My Ugandan friend had every assurance that he had been born because he was alive. Recollection isn't necessary. I have no memory whatever of my physical birth, but I know I was born because I'm alive. Pinch me and I hurt. Cut me and I bleed. Reject me and I feel emotional pain. The vital signs of life, physically and emotionally, attest to the reality of my birth.

The same is true with spiritual life. The new birth cannot be reduced to some particular formula or type of experience. One need have no recollection of some conversion experience to affirm being born again. I certainly don't have to produce a spiritual birth certificate to prove that I've been born again. The insistence of my accoster in the bookstore that I give the date and description of being born again was unreasonable and unnecessary. As Jesus said to Nicodemus, "The wind blows wherever it pleases. You hear its sound, but you cannot tell where it comes from or where it is going. So it is with everyone born of the Spirit" (John 3:8). Let us celebrate the mystery of the new birth by enjoying the fact that it cannot be reduced to definitions and categories!

As with physical life, the evidence of the spiritual new birth is the presence of life. There are numerous vital signs of spiritual life, but perhaps the most basic is an awareness of God that centers in Jesus Christ. One who has been born again becomes consciously aware of the love and the presence of God and, most likely, develops some practices through prayer and Bible reading to enhance and expand that awareness into all the activities and seasons of life.

Certainly, the new birth produces an entirely different way of looking at the world. Values change. Things that were very important often become less important. Things previously ignored or neglected become central. Archbishop William Temple once said that the world is like a gigantic department store where someone entered during the night and reversed all the price tags, putting high prices on things of low value. When a person is born again, the price tags are rightly rearranged. And I experience this as an ongoing process. My sensitivities to the values of God's Kingdom are ever growing, even if all too slowly sometimes!

The new birth, then, produces a unique view of the importance of loving relationships with those around us and with those whom we will probably never meet. In fact, this new birth enables us to love our enemies. Back in the dark days of Idi Amin's destructive rule of terror in Uganda, someone asked Bishop Festo Kivengere what he would do if he were handed a loaded revolver in Amin's presence. Unwaveringly Festo indicated that he would say, "I believe that this is your weapon, Mr. Amin, not mine. My weapon is love."

There is no need for any of us to run around adver-
tising our vital signs of spiritual life. Realistically, we
know all too well that we daily miss the mark of what God
made us to be. Yet as we experience the signs and wonders
of life in Christ, let us affirm with joy and thankfulness
that we are born again by God's grace. Our routes to
conversion may have been slightly different but we all
journey in Christ.

4

CONVERSION

Unfortunately, conversion . . . is often regarded as a particular type of experience rather than a process of being made useful for the Kingdom . . . the process will take different forms and shapes for different folks . . .

Converted people are given the gift of a new focus, an ability to see things as they really are in terms of the Kingdom of God, and to live in the conscious awareness of Jesus' love and presence, even in the times of suffering and despair.

WITHOUT COMMENT, Vin Scully, the renowned dean of major league baseball announcers, referred to a Dodger pitcher as a converted outfielder. In this case, the appropriate response was not "Praise the Lord!" Scully was not describing the young athlete's spiritual condition; he was simply pointing out that the pitcher had once played in the outfield but had changed positions on the diamond.

The other day I read a fascinating article in a business journal on the conversion of salt water into fresh water. There was no suggestion that this had anything to do with a need for salt water to undergo a spiritual transformation; rather the article described current research in this field and emphasized the speculative aspects of related investments.

Perhaps more than any other word in our Christian

vocabulary, "conversion" is used universally with a casual matter-of-factness. I'm writing this chapter enroute from Nairobi to Amsterdam to Los Angeles, a trip that has a way of feeling like a marathon. During the past two weeks, I have been speaking to pastors in four different African countries. The conversion of currency is a way of life on such trips—especially in countries like Kenya and Zimbabwe, which have very strict rules on foreign exchange. There it is illegal to convert foreign currency except at banks and recognized hotels. So the standard procedure upon arrival is to make your first stop, after clearing customs, at the "Change" window to convert your dollars into local currency. Your dollars are not legal tender, and thus not useful, until they have been converted.

This gets us to the basic idea of conversion. Conversion is changing someone or something in order to create usefulness. An outfielder is not useful as a pitcher until he has undergone a remarkable process of change in his abilities to throw and field the ball. Salt water is not useful for quenching thirst. As a matter of fact, drinking it can be fatal, as people stranded on the high seas have painfully experienced. How strange that one can die of thirst in the middle of a vast ocean of water! And you may have a pocketful of U.S. dollars in Zimbabwe or Kenya, but they aren't useful in simple commerce until they have been converted into Zimbabwe dollars or Kenya shillings.

Nicodemus Revisited

It's the same with the Kingdom of God. People are useful for all kinds of things, but to be useful in God's Kingdom, they have to undergo a thorough conversion. Let's go back to Nicodemus, whom we met in the previous chapter on being born again. You will recall in John 3 that remarkable conversation between him and Jesus. As we saw, Nicodemus was a good man, a Pharisee and a member of the Sanhedrin, the ruling body of the Jewish nation. Obviously, Nicodemus was a very useful man in many ways. He was certainly instrumental to his community as a dedicated leader and upstanding citizen. He was obviously esteemed in the temple as a devout man of God and a leader in its work and worship. Finally, there could be little question that he was a devoted husband and father, for exemplary family life was required of Sanhedrin members.

How difficult it must have been for this very useful man to grasp his need for radical (in the sense of *root* or *basic*) and thorough change in order to be useful in the Kingdom of God. Both the demand for and the offer of the new birth to Nicodemus indicates that, in the thinking of Jesus, Nicodemus needed to be converted in order to have real life—life in the Kingdom.

The same theme was articulated by Jesus in response to the question asked by the disciples, "Who is the greatest in the kingdom of heaven?" (Matt. 18:1).

Bringing a little child into their midst, he said, "Unless you change and become like little children, you will never enter the kingdom of heaven" (Matt. 18:3).

Nothing is more basic than this theme of conversion. To be useful to God, one must be converted.

What Conversion Is

Unfortunately, conversion to Christ is often regarded as a particular type of experience rather than a process of being made useful for the Kingdom. This is not to say that the process may not be sudden and dramatic for some. But it is to insist that the process will take different forms and shapes for different folks.

To stereotype conversion into an identifiable experience is just plain wrong! Look at Paul and Timothy, for example. Paul's conversion began with as dramatic an experience as one could ever imagine. The story is told in Acts 9:1–19. On his way to Damascus to kill some more Christians (believing this to be expedient for the Kingdom of God), Saul is confronted personally by Jesus Himself. Blinded and numbed, Paul spent three days in what must have been awesome bewilderment. After the visit of Ananias, though, Saul became Paul, a powerful man in the Kingdom of God. What a conversion experience!

Timothy represents quite a contrast. When Paul wrote to his young son in the faith, he cited no blinding encounters or dazzling visions but rather affirmed what had been a lifelong process. "I have been reminded of your sincere faith, which first lived in your grandmother Lois and in your mother Eunice and, I am persuaded, now lives in you also" (2 Tim. 1:5). Probably Timothy was nurtured in a climate of faith in which trust in Christ came as a natural part of his life. It wasn't grandmother's or mother's faith that saved him, but his own faith grew out of their witness and example. To Timothy, conversion had been a lifelong process. To Paul it had been an identifiable crisis. But both were converted.

I'm surrounded by folks who relate different types of conversion processes. There's Dick Leon, a highly regarded Presbyterian pastor in the Pacific Northwest. I first knew Dick when he was student body president at the University of Washington in Seattle. Billy Graham was in town for a crusade, and as Minister of Youth at the University Presbyterian Church I had agreed to spearhead an effort to get a large delegation of UW students to one of the evening sessions. Dick came to the service, largely out of curiosity, for he had never indicated any interest in this kind of thing. When the invitation was given, I was delighted to see Dick go forward as an inquirer. Right then he opened his life to Christ, accepted Him as Savior and Lord, and has never doubted his conversion to Christ that night more than thirty years ago.

Donn Moomaw, pastor of a thriving congregation in Los Angeles, the Bel Air Presbyterian Church, had a similar but different conversion. Donn was raised in a home with deeply dedicated Christian parents. And they had been raised by Christian parents. Although Donn had grown up in Sunday school and church, he never quite got around to any serious commitment to Christ, perhaps because football was his whole life. A nationally sought-after linebacker, he chose to play at UCLA, where he was given every possible honor, the ultimate being his induction into the College Football Hall of Fame a few years ago.

Donn will admit that while he certainly knew the basics of the Christian faith from childhood, he was of no use to the Kingdom. He will also tell you that on a particular Saturday evening in the apartment of a Los Angeles businessman, after playing one of the best games of his life, against USC no less, he opened his life to Christ, praying a simple prayer of commitment. Since that Saturday night, more than thirty years ago, Donn has been a useful citizen of the Kingdom. In one sense, his conversion was a lifelong process, beginning with Christian parents and grandparents. But in another sense, his conversion happened at a particular time and place.

Marily Evans Demarest, my wife of more than twenty-five years, is one of the most useful people in the Kingdom I know. I have watched her beautiful influence upon our four daughters across the years. They have received her loving care and devotion all this time. In addition, there is the quiet and strong help that she brings to innumerable people year upon year. All this places her high on my list of those unsung heroes of the Kingdom.

If you ask Marily about her conversion "experience," you'll draw a blank, for, like Timothy, she never had one. For her, conversion has been a lifelong process. She'll tell you that she can't recall a time in her life when she hasn't loved Christ and trusted Him as Savior and Lord. And many times, she heard her preacher-father, Dr. Louis H. Evans, insist to a congregation that "being born in a Christian home doesn't make you into a Christian any more than being born in a garage makes you into an automobile." Marily has always known that it was *her* faith, not her father's, nor her mother's, nor her grandparents', but she can't recall when that faith began. She'll tell you that she's been converted, and everyone who knows her will affirm it. But she can't tell you when.

My own journey is yet another story. I was raised by parents who certainly knew and loved Christ, but for whom the church and Christian activities were marginal. As a freshman in high school, I was baptized in a Baptist church during a week of meetings conducted by a visiting evangelist. But during my high school years, the stint in the Marine Corps during World War II, and the time until my senior year at Cal Berkeley, my faith and Christian commitment were a matter of ups-and-downs, with the downs ahead by a margin of ten to one!

Most people who knew me then would not have identified me as a follower of Christ.

During my last year in college, I was drawn to a new, young pastor at the First Presbyterian Church of Berkeley, Dr. Robert Boyd Munger. I was invited to share in a small group of men who met with Dr. Munger for Bible study each Saturday morning. Before my senior year was over, I had begun to experience Christ, really and personally, as never before. Within a few months of graduation, I felt strongly led by Him to leave my fledgling career as a civil engineer and to study for the ministry. In one sense, I had no conversion "experience," but instead, a long process culminated over a six-month period in 1947 that led to my becoming a useful citizen of the Kingdom.

To borrow the title of William James' book, there are many "varieties of religious experience," any or all of which can be authentic and life-changing. But we do well to keep Christian conversion separate from particular "experiences" and to think of conversion as a process, whether sudden or prolonged.

What Conversion Does

Important as it is to think of conversion as a process rather than a particular type of experience, the best way to focus upon the meaning of conversion is to view its results. Conversion always produces tangible results, however imperfect, in a person's life and relationships.

A New Focus

Conversion always produces a new focus in one's thinking and living. Conversion results in a turning to God. God increasingly is center stage in one's thinking, and the hunger for His life is an increasing part of one's consciousness. Thus the universal witness of Kingdom people down through the ages are regular times spent in prayer and Bible reading. Hours and days spent apart from conscious communion with God become desert places in the otherwise verdant pastures of our lives in Christ.

Our places of work, with their routine and often humdrum schedules and activities, become the settings for living out the drama of the Kingdom. We grow in our sensitivity to those around us, and in our desire to respond to every person as Jesus Himself would respond. We try, we fail, and we try again. And when we do succeed, we recognize the power of Jesus at work in us. This new focus makes the whole world look different. I recall a little poster over the kitchen sink in one particular home where I was visiting. It said simply, "Divine services held here three times each day." When the menial task of washing dishes becomes filled with the sense of God's presence, we see a sure sign of genuine conversion!

As an avid amateur photographer, I look forward to receiving each issue of a photography magazine. Its section on new products continually boggles my mind. Who would have dreamed ten years ago that today we would have cameras with automatic everything? Because some of us like to have a little more say about what we get in a picture, they've obliged us by developing added technology to override the fine-tuned technology!

One of the critical things in photography, automatic or otherwise, is focus. And focus includes depth-of-field. Depth-of-field alludes to the distance from the camera in which the subject is in focus. A long depth-of-field means that everything from up close to far away will be in focus. A short depth-of-field means that only those objects within a particular range (for example, from ten to fourteen feet) will be in focus. With newer films and cameras, we now have much greater flexibility with depth-of-field, and with the right combination of film and camera, one can readily take pictures with everything, up close and far away, in perfect focus.

Conversion to Christ enables us to keep everything in focus. He helps us keep things in perspective without anything getting blurred. As I said, I'm writing while returning home from another trip to Africa. I've just spent three days with forty pastors in Kampala, Uganda. Three weeks ago, the streets of Kampala were a combat zone as Museveni's troops expelled Okello, who six months ago expelled Obote, who had expelled Amin, who had expelled Obote. The full measure of the atrocities and tragedies experienced by the people of Uganda over the past twenty years will probably never be known.

But as I have been visiting with pastors and people in Uganda in recent years, I have been overwhelmed with their ability to keep things in focus. In this moment, the pastors with whom I met are celebrating Museveni's overthrow of Okello. They believe that Museveni represents their best chance for healing this broken and embattled little country. Much better days are ahead, they believe. But they were just as radiant in their faith and lives in the dark days under Amin and Obote as they are now! That's what I call depth-of-field, keeping everything in focus.

Converted people are given the gift of a new focus, an ability to see things as they really are in terms of the Kingdom of God, and to live in the conscious awareness of Jesus' love and presence, even in the times of suffering and despair.

A New Sense of Values

Conversion is a process in which our values are always being tested and reexamined. And this is a never-ending process. Getting away from America from time to time and seeing ourselves through the eyes of other believers in other cultures requires that kind of reexamination within me like nothing else I do. We American Christians tend to be so cocksure of ourselves! Whether liberal or conservative, we feel that we have the final say in all matters, biblical and theological. We consider our

THE HEART OF THE FAITH

political and economic system to be virtually synonymous with the Kingdom of God. And our lifestyle of lavish consumption is too often regarded as a sign of God's
blessing.

While we rightly express our indignation at apart-
heid in South Africa, let's put our protest in proper perspective. As we attack their distorted values, let's open
up an examination of our own. As their value system
must be open to the critique of the entire world, so must
ours. And let's not forget our brothers and sisters there
who *have* reexamined their values and who *are* taking
their stand against the government in its stubborn de-
fense of an indefensible doctrine. I must be as willing to
reexamine my values as they have theirs.

And what are some of our personal and collective
values that need closer scrutiny? Conversion requires
reappraisal of our views of wealth and property. What
possibly can continue to justify our extravagant consumption when vast numbers of our Christian sisters and
brothers are in such desperate need? Some serious study
of 2 Corinthians 8 and 9 is long overdue.

Finally, conversion calls for a reexamination of our
commitments and responsibilities in personal relationships. In our passion for self-fulfillment, we're trampling
each other to death. Brokenness at every level of human
relationships is all too typical. As a pastor, I'm seeing it
practically every day. How are we going to relate our
virtual idolization of self-fulfillment with the One whose
first word is the call for us to deny ourselves?

A New Usefulness

I've placed much of the emphasis on conversion upon usefulness. Whether it's a baseball outfielder, salt water, or the dollar, conversion has to do with making someone or something useful.

The shortest of Paul's letters in the New Testament is also a much-neglected one. Philemon was written as a personal letter from Paul during his Roman imprisonment to Philemon, a friend of apparent means. Philemon's slave had run away and somehow had come into the orbit of Paul in Rome. Conversion has a way of making you want to make past wrongs right whenever possible. Onesimus clearly needed to make amends to his former owner and master, now his brother in Christ. That's a scary thing to face. So Paul graciously wrote a letter, affirming Onesimus's conversion and virtually demanding that Philemon offer forgiveness and acceptance to his new brother in Christ.

At midpoint in Paul's letter, he captured the essence of true conversion: "I appeal to you for my son Onesimus, who became my son while I was in chains. Formerly he was useless to you, but now he has become useful both to you and to me" (Philem. 10, 11).

The clever play on words comes through even in English translation. In Greek, the word "Onesimus" means *useful*. As a runaway, he had been useless to Philemon, but now as a converted Brother, he was truly Onesimus, truly useful.

And that's what conversion is all about. It may or may not be tied to specific types of religious experiences. It may begin in an identifiable moment, or it may transpire over longer periods of time. It is best defined by its products in one's thinking, living, and relationships.

Blessed indeed are those who have been, and are being, *converted*!

5

SANCTIFICATION

We must get beyond regarding sanctification merely or even primarily as personal piety. Once we establish the standards by which we determine who the "good Christians" are, we have set up unavoidable divisions. We can recover the biblical meaning of sanctification only by returning to the root idea of holiness as being a people "set apart" for the worship and service of God.

Therefore, since through God's mercy we have this ministry, we do not lose heart. Rather, we have renounced secret and shameful ways; we do not use deception, nor do we distort the word of God. On the contrary, by setting forth the truth plainly we commend ourselves to every man's conscience in the sight of God.

. . . we have this treasure in jars of clay to show that this all-surpassing power is from God and not from us. We are hard pressed on every side, but not crushed; perplexed, but not in despair; persecuted, but not abandoned; struck down, but not destroyed. We always carry around in our body the death of Jesus, so that the life of Jesus may also be revealed in our body. For we who are alive are always being given over to death for Jesus' sake, so that his life may be revealed in our mortal body.   (2 Cor 4:1, 2; 7–11)

Although the word isn't used in this passage, Paul is writing about what we call "sanctification." Now I have to confess that *sanctification* is a term I would like to abolish from our Christian vocabulary.

If you're familiar with Christian words, what comes to your mind when you hear the word "sanctification"? Some might say, "Huh? What's that?" Others wince or shudder. All too often this term conjures a picture of a holier-than-thou type ever ready to pounce on us when we fail to measure up to his or her predetermined standards for the behavior of "good" Christians.

In reality, we really can't throw the word "sanctification" out because it is deeply rooted and imbedded in the writings of Scripture. We just can't take the Bible seriously without at least knowing what it means. *Sanctify* and *sanctification* come from the word for "holy." The idea of holiness is, of course, central to the writers of the Bible.

Throughout Scripture, holiness is portrayed as an essential attribute of God. In saying that God is holy, we are affirming that God is different from everything else in His creation. To be holy is to be set apart. Holiness and separateness are synonymous terms. That's why some theologians speak of God as "Wholly Other."

A companion idea to the holiness of God is that of the holiness of God's people. "I am the Lord who brought you up out of Egypt to be your God; therefore be holy, because I am holy" (Lev. 11:45). The story of God's people is the story of human beings called by God to share in His holiness—to be set apart for God's worship and service.

All too often, the holiness of God's people has been thought of only in terms of personal piety. And this assumption often has bred a legalism and judgmentalism that has been the source of division and brokenness within the church. Instead of a community of people who genuinely care for each other and regularly bear one another's burdens, we create communities of people majoring in gossip and criticism. The result, tragically, is the denial of the very grace which Christ gives us.

We must get beyond regarding sanctification merely or even primarily as personal piety. Once we establish the standards by which we determine who the "good Christians" are, we have set up unavoidable divisions. We can recover the biblical meaning of sanctification only by returning to the root idea of holiness as being a people "set apart" for the worship and service of God.

Sanctification is not an achievement for a few spiritual superstars who excel in piety, but a lifelong process engaging the everyday lives of all believers. Paul sums up his view of sanctification without ever using the word:

> Not that I have already obtained all this, or have already been made perfect, but I press on to take hold of that for which Christ Jesus took hold of me. Brothers, I do not consider myself yet to have taken hold of it. But one thing I do: Forgetting what is behind and straining toward what is ahead, I press on toward the goal to win the prize for which God has called me heavenward in Christ Jesus.
>
> (Phil. 3:12–14)

Sanctification in Action

There is a marvelous section in the *Form of Government* of the Presbyterian Church, U.S.A., which describes the meaning of church membership in ways which are applicable to us all:

A faithful member accepts Christ's call to be involved responsibly in the ministry of his church. Such involvement includes:

proclaiming the good news,

taking part in the common life and worship of a particular church,

praying and studying Scripture and the faith of the Christian church,

supporting the work of the church through the giving of money, time, and talents,

participating in the governing responsibilities of the church,

demonstrating a new quality of life within and through the church,

responding to God's activity in the world through service to others,

living responsibly in the personal, family, voca-
tional, political, cultural, and social relationships of life,

working in the world for peace, justice, freedom, and human fulfillment.

Involvement in such a lifestyle requires a high level
of commitment by the church member but produces a
great sense of meaning and joyous satisfaction for him
or her.

The reality, though, is that all who aspire to such
lofty spiritual goals are in for frustration and discour-
agement.

I'm reminded of the description of Pastor Fleming in
A. J. Cronin's novel, *Beyond This Place:* "It was his
tragedy that he longed to be a Saint, a true disciple who
would heal by his touch, make his flock radiant with
the Word of God, which he himself felt so deeply. He
wanted to soar. But alas, his tongue was clumsy, his feet
bogged—he was earthbound."

Every one of us who has ever attempted to be
a leader, servant, minister, elder, deacon . . . and responsible member of the church of Jesus Christ knows
Cronin's description well. No matter how hard we try, we
are clearly more sinner than saint. Just when we would
soar into heavenly fantasy, we find ourselves earthbound!

This is precisely Paul's testimony to his own ministry in our text:

we who have this spiritual treasure are like common
clay pots . . .

we are often troubled, but never crushed;

sometimes in doubt, but never in despair;

there are many enemies, but we are never without a
friend;

and though badly hurt at times, we are not destroyed.

At all times we carry in our mortal bodies the death
of Jesus, so that His life also may be seen in our
bodies.

This picture of hardship, struggle, and suffering for
the sake of responsible church membership and ministry
is far removed from actual practice in our contemporary
world. The outward success of many churches belies the
fact that we in the American churches are actually in
rapid decline, both in numbers and influence.

We hear rumors of a revival of religion in America,
especially of the evangelical variety; but statistics tell a
different story. North America and Europe were more
Christian in our great-grandparents' day than in ours.
Since 1900, according to the *World Christian Encyclopedia*, "massive defections from Christianity" of secularists
in Western Europe, communists in Russia and Eastern
Europe, and materialists in the Americas, have made the
fastest–growing religion in the West not Christianity,

and not one of the other great world religions, but *no religion*. Professed non-religion in America is growing six-and-one-half times faster than Christianity; in Europe, twelve times faster. "Every year, 2,765,000 church attenders in Europe and North America cease to be practicing Christians . . . an average loss of 7,600 every day."

A *Los Angeles Times* poll recently indicated that thirty percent of Americans surveyed said they "almost never" go to church or synagogue services. That figure has more than doubled in the past five years from fourteen percent.

It will take a *new church*—local churches that are experiencing genuine renewal by the power of God—to be faithful witnesses and servants in the midst of decay and decline. And this new church can be the product only of a new breed of leader-members, members who will discover the sheer joy of taking their membership and their ministry with lively seriousness.

Two Perils

Paul's testimony long ago gives us some clues as to what this kind of renewal might look like by describing without flinching the realities that confront every person who dares to take Jesus at His word.

The church in America is confronted today with two grave perils: *despair* and *false hope*.

I see Paul's metaphor of the "earthen vessels" or "common clay pots" in 2 Corinthians 4:7 as a vivid picture of these perils. The NIV translation reads, "But we have this treasure in jars of clay to show that this all-surpassing power is from God and not from us."

The peril of *despair* becomes a reality when we recognize the frailty of our "clay pots." Here we are back at Pastor Fleming's problem. The simple reality is ever present. We are not as strong and invincible as we would like to believe. We can bluff, brag, and push; we can work nobly to reinforce our weak self-images; we can make lavish displays of pomp and circumstance; but we cannot escape our fears and weaknesses. Somewhere we must recognize that we share a kinship with all other physical creatures, a kinship that unites us in death.

It was the Greek philosopher Diogenes, second in renown only to Alexander the Great, who espoused the way of *Cynicism*. The word "cynic" comes from the Greek word *kunikos,* which means "dog-like." The cynics believed we should recognize the fact that we are simply animals, give up our high expectations and hopes, and live "naturally." They refused to amass goods and properties and scoffed at every system of meaning and every institution which assumed unique values for human beings. One such scholar summed up this cynical message to humanity as: "*Fear nothing, desire nothing, possess nothing, and then Life, with all its ingenuity of malice, cannot disappoint you.*"

Cynicism seems to have taken a new twist in our day by withdrawing from the outer world into the inner world. Having given up our hope for the world of society, for the global community, and for the human race, we turn in upon ourselves with a new set of hopes and dreams. We work at being beautiful and young; we jog; we do aerobics; we escape with our walkmans and video movies. We surround ourselves with every new comfort and luxury. We even develop spiritual techniques to assure our ultimate happiness—in fact, God is regarded as being primarily concerned with our personal wellbeing and good fortune. But ultimately, this strategy backfires, for when our strategies for self-fulfillment fail to deliver us from the hard realities of life in a fallen world, we end up blaming God for our unhappiness. Our despair is all the greater.

But all too readily we try to counter the threat of despair by raising *false hopes*. While recognizing the frailty of our clay pots, we must be on guard against *denying* our weakness and frailty by closing our eyes to the world of reality, believing only what we want to believe, striving to make the clay pots invincible. I am convinced that much of what is set forth in the name of Christianity in America today is grounded more in our false hopes and illusions than in the message of Jesus.

Jesus, church membership, and Christian living are widely presented as a means to self-fulfillment and happiness. The world of the evangelical Christian becomes a world of promised success based on the experiences of Christian celebrities who have succeeded in acquiring fame and wealth. It offers miracles and instant healing on a much wider scale than did Jesus Himself, primarily to deliver people from all unhappiness, real or imagined. It invites young and old to withdraw into the safe world of spirituality, promising peace of mind, victory over sin and evil, and security in this life and the next.

It should not surprise us that the movement from one peril to the other is so frequent. How often we witness the dramatic conversion from one to the other—and sadly, the movement goes in both directions. How we celebrate the conversion from despair to false hope! But how dumbstruck we are when the one we have known as a "radiant Christian" (of the false hope variety) drops out of the fold.

The sheer beauty and joy of Paul's testimony to us in our text enables us to avoid either peril: *we have this treasure in jars of clay.*

We affirm and recognize our frailty. We keep close tabs on our expectations, checking them when they become unrealistic but never giving up all hope.

We accept pain and suffering as a part of life, but we never confuse the common clay pot with the treasure that God has put in it.

We will give in neither to the death of all expectation nor to the lure of happiness and security.

With Paul,

We will be troubled, but never crushed;

We will be sometimes in doubt, but never in despair

We will have many enemies, but never be without a friend;

We will be badly hurt at times, but never destroyed.

It is members who have this perspective who will produce the renewed church that is so needed in our land in this hour. But leaders are desperately needed to call the church to costly, genuine sacrificial service.

To those who will pay the price involved in living between the two perils of despair and false hope, the future is filled with hope. Such will be the new leaders for a new church. Such is the process of sanctification. It is the ongoing journey of those who choose to be servants and followers of Jesus within His body, the church.

The armchair philosopher, Jess Lair, entitled one of his delightful books *I Ain't Well, But I Sure Am Better.* For the disciple of Jesus Christ, this is an apt description of sanctification. And when Dr. Lair asks the question, "Why does Paul call me a saint, when my closest friend knows I ain't?" we can answer, "Because that's what sanctification is all about!"

Every day we can celebrate the reality that in good times and in bad times, in success and failure, in strength and in weakness, we are all together in this process. We *are* becoming useful instruments for the worship and service of God.

6

COMMITMENT

. . . there's a radical difference between commitment based upon what appears to be personal advantage and commitment based upon one's willingness to become a giver, not a taker.

WHILE *COMMITMENT* is a term not used extensively in the Bible, it is certainly a word basic to our understanding and experience of the Christian faith. Nowhere is the power of commitment more beautifully expressed than in Psalm 37:

Trust in the Lord and do good;
  dwell in the land and enjoy safe pasture.
Delight yourself in the Lord
  and he will give you the desires of your heart.
Commit your way to the Lord;
  trust in him and he will do this:
He will make your righteousness shine like the dawn,
  the justice of your cause like the noonday sun.
                                        (Psalm 37:3–6)

In an obvious oversimplification, a friend of mine insists that there are only two kinds of people in the world: givers and takers. And he's quick to warn about putting too much trust in those takers. And yet, with alarming increase, our prevailing strategies for living are based upon getting rather than giving.

I'm concerned lest, in the interest of making the gospel of Jesus Christ relevant, we invite people to accept Him as Savior and Lord in order for them to get what they want—or feel they need. This may well attract more folks to church, but it will never produce disciples.

Wasn't personal gratification the issue after Jesus had fed the large crowd? He had multiplied the meager lunch of the lad, the crowd ate their fill, and there was food to spare. Needless to say, many of those men and women on the hillside that day realized the potential of this kind of power. Who wouldn't want to have a source of plentiful food available? Who wouldn't want to have such a doer of deeds ever present? With such demonstrable power, it shouldn't be too difficult to get a following!

As the people clamored for Christ, He withdrew "into the hills by himself" (John 6:15). When He crossed the Sea of Galilee the next day it was certainly predictable that the crowds who had been fed the day before would do their best to find Him. They did, and were confronted by His strong warning: "I tell you the truth, you are looking for me, not because you saw miraculous signs but because you ate the loaves and had your fill" (John 6:26).

Had they seen the miraculous sign as evidence that

the Kingdom of God had broken into this age, their motives for following Christ would have been entirely different. But as it was, they saw only the material advantage that could be theirs through His power. Is it any wonder that Jesus rebuked them for their selfish motives? You see, there's a radical difference between commitment based upon what appears to be personal advantage and commitment based upon one's willingness to become a giver, not a taker.

I can't resist the story of the chicken and the pig. After they had enjoyed a brief visit, the chicken suggested that they get together for a more relaxed encounter. "Why don't you come to my place for breakfast tomorrow? You bring the ham, and I'll supply the eggs." "No way!" said the pig. "For you that's convenience; but for me, it's total commitment!"

Somehow we've gotten the idea that Christian commitment is a matter of convenience, when in reality it's a call to total submission. To accommodate the gospel to a culture that majors in self-fulfillment is to betray it.

The Call to Commitment

The story of the Bible is the story of God's continuing love and search for men and women. It's not so much a matter of our finding God as it is of His finding us. After the initial disobedience in the Garden of Eden, it was God who took the initiative toward reconciliation and forgiveness. It was He who called, "Where are you?"

From the beginning, the theme is the same—God is always looking for you and me.

As God seeks us, He is always calling us to costly commitment. The story of Abraham in Genesis 12 unfolds the drama of redemptive history that reaches its culmination in Jesus. The beginning of this story of redemption begins with a call to commitment: "The Lord said to Abram, 'Leave your country, your people and your father's household and go to the land I will show you'" (Gen. 12:1).

God's call demands a total reorientation of Abraham's life and relationships. It is a call into the unknown, to new places and responsibilities. If he obeys, Abraham will find himself in situations where only God can sustain him. Abraham is free to stay where he is with his accrued securities or to venture into the uncertain with certainty only in God. The venture into the unknown is the journey of faith, and it can be neither started nor sustained apart from an intentional and long-term commitment.

I wish I could tell you that I can identify fully with Abraham, but I can't. I can't say that God's call to me has been as explicit or as costly. I've never felt my commitment to Christ demanded that I leave for a task and unknown places with my immediate family and possessions. Yet I'm certainly aware that God calls me to a commitment just as total as Abraham's.

This call to total commitment takes different

shapes and forms throughout the Bible. The prophet Micah, for example, expressed God's call in the well-known statement: "He has showed you, O man, what is good. And what does the Lord require of you? To act justly and to love mercy and to walk humbly with your God" (Micah 6:8).

"To act justly" requires costly obedience in many situations. Our brothers and sisters in South Africa, black and white, know much more about this than I, as do countless others in many other places.

"To love mercy" requires a willingness to forgive and to enter into the pain of others that can be very costly indeed. This phrase always takes me to the foot of the cross, hearing once again, "Father, forgive them, for they do not know what they are doing."

"To walk humbly with God" is not all that easy when living in a society that justifies just about anything, once it is defined as a personal need. Nor does the interpretation of material abundance as a sure sign of God's blessing lead to this kind of humility.

The prophet Amos challenges those who believe that the performance of external religious exercises fulfils God's call to commitment. Amos echoes the confrontation as it came from God: "I hate, I despise your religious feasts; I cannot stand your assemblies. Even though you bring me burnt offerings and grain offerings, I will not accept them. Though you bring choice fellowship offerings, I will have no regard for them. Away with the noise of your songs! I will not listen to the music of your harps. But let justice roll on like a river, righteousness like a never-failing stream!" (5:21–24).

God's call to commitment is much more than one to perform religious duties. How absurd that we continue to debate the question as to whether or not the church should be involved in anything other than religious activities, or whether the individual Christian should be involved in anything other than spiritual growth! Any separation between the spiritual life and devotion to justice and righteousness is foreign to the Bible. And it takes a strong, intentional commitment to be faithful in both arenas.

Jesus certainly made the issue clear to the rich young ruler: "Sell everything you have and give to the poor . . . . Then come, follow me" (Luke 18:22). While there is probably no need to apply this imperative to every person universally as though it were the eleventh commandment, those of us basking in the midst of affluence must take a good look at the substance of the issue involved.

In the priorities of his wealth and power, this young man was still seeking for the meaning of "eternal life." The essence of life was lacking, although he certainly had every reason to celebrate success. He had practiced traditional morality to perfection, but it wasn't enough. The diagnosis of Jesus was direct and to the point.

The young man's basic problem was his unwillingness to commit to anything that was not in his best interests as measured from the standpoint of material security and wellbeing. This is the potential tragedy of affluence. It has a way of becoming a pseudo-faith in a way of life.

I think often of the many Christians I have come to know and love in Uganda. Since the early 1970s, when Idi Amin seized control of the government, Ugandans have experienced incredible suffering. Under both Amin and Obote, thousands of citizens were imprisoned, tortured, and killed for their stubborn commitment to follow Jesus—whatever the cost.

Recently I returned from five days in Kabale, where twenty thousand Ugandans, Rwandans, Tanzanians, and Kenyans gathered for the celebration of the fiftieth anniversary of the beginning of the East African Revival, a continuing working of the Holy Spirit that has sustained them through hardship and poverty.

To experience their incredible poverty firsthand, to touch the inescapable routineness and simplicity of their lives, and to hear some of them recite their stories of atrocities—these stories of their persecution threaten me with self-contempt. These people don't sit around complaining about the things I do; nor do they spend the hours that I do contemplating the psychology of belief. In a very real sense, their circumstances have simplified their philosophy. They have experienced evil in its raw and brute force; they have seen the most extreme consequences of life lived without regard for God or human wellbeing. For them, commitment to Christ is not a matter of frosting on the cake. It *is* the cake.

The tension I feel in the presence of these brothers and sisters is very real. On the one hand, I ache for them in the midst of their hardships and deprivation. Surely God's children deserve much better! But on the other hand, I envy them in their joyous, reckless abandon to the life of faith. In their presence I am acutely aware of what affluence is doing to me. Somehow I feel especially akin to that rich young ruler who went away "sorrowful."

The fear of risk, the fear of commitment to something which might cost a lifestyle is overpowering. If Jesus were to say to me what He said to the young man, I, too, might disappoint Christ rather than forfeit the very things I have come to trust.

Barriers to Commitment

If I really believe that Christ is "the way, the truth, and the life," and that He calls me to follow Him at the risk of losing everything else, I am faced with a momentous choice. I must choose to give up everything for His sake, or I will try to hold on to what I have and go through the motions of being "Christian" to gain His acceptance and support.

Perhaps for those of us in the developed countries, the greatest barrier to genuine commitment is our relative affluence. We feel we have worked too long and hard to get what we have to hazard losing it. To commit to One who affirms that "it is more blessed to give than to receive" (Acts 20:35) does not easily fit into our categories.

We prefer our material and physical security above all else, and we play it safe all around. The idea of finding ourselves by losing ourselves is ultimately foreign to our best-laid strategies for self-fulfillment.

Another major barrier to venturous commitment to God is our accepted pattern of calculating the outcome of every decision we make. Our fear of loss is ever present and all too often controlling. Now understand I'm not equating the call to Christian commitment with stupidity or naiveté. When purchasing an automobile or making an investment, we best ask the right questions and have the proper assurances of the wisdom of those decisions. While the risk of commitment is never grounded in gullibility, our incessant desire to have every assurance of security or success before we move out in trust is nevertheless a deterrent to commitment.

No one can tell you what commitment to Christ will be like. It comes differently for every individual. Don't confuse commitment with doing "great things" for God, though. When I bring the challenge of commitment to people in Uganda, I have little reason to believe that simple, remote villagers in East Africa will ever become great world leaders in the Kingdom of God. But neither do I know whether one of them may become another Bishop Festo Kivengere, a Ugandan high school teacher whose commitment led to his becoming a strong voice in international Christian leadership. It really doesn't matter. In the Kingdom of God the least are the greatest; the greatest are the least; the weak are the strong; and the

strong are the weak. Human ways of measuring signif-
icance and insignificance do not apply in God's Kingdom.

There is no guarantee that your commitment to
Christ will insure health, wealth, and prosperity to you or
to anyone else. The issue at stake is neither security nor
success. The issue is one of fidelity to the God who loves
you. Your commitment might mean that you will end up
much poorer in material things. Or it may mean that you
will become less and less accepted by your peers.

This has been especially hard for me. Looking back,
I know that popularity has always been important in my
life. I doubt that I would have invested so much time and
energy in becoming Student Body President at Cal
Berkeley if that weren't the case. After becoming a Christian, I experienced warm acceptance in the Christian
community. I was called upon often to give my testimony
to my new commitment to Christ. Soon I was being en-
couraged to prepare for the ministry. At every point, I
found widespread acceptance and encouragement. Although I don't question that the ministry has been God's
specific call for my life, I can see that the popularity
factor was present in that commitment.

Does awareness of acceptance make my commitment wrong? Not at all. But it has certainly forced me
to re-think what ministry really is. Decisions must not
be made on the basis of "how they'll play in Peoria."
Sermons mustn't be shaped with opinion polls in mind.
To follow Jesus with integrity, especially in a community of affluence, will inevitably require some unpopu-
lar stands on social issues and some forthright actions

when people would rather be uninvolved. In short, pastors and people are called to be faithful, not merely to be "Who's Who" entries.

Getting Off the Dime

I've always been a procrastinator. Even as a child, I put off things until the last minute. As a matter of fact, I'm finishing this book already past the agreed-upon deadline! I even bought a book on procrastination, and I fully intend to read it—next week!

My dad, on the other hand, was a great believer in the "do-it-now" way of life. For him it was quite simple. If something was supposed to be done, *do it now!* One of his most-used phrases with me was "Get off the dime!" I never asked him what he meant.

For most of us, the issue isn't knowing or believing that we ought to be making more serious moves toward greater commitment of ourselves to the living God. I think the issue is getting off the dime.

And those of us who are procrastinating in that commitment are in good company. Moses, who became the great leader of Israel, also had a problem with postponement.

The story of God's call to Moses is delightfully narrated in Exodus 3 and 4. Moses, who has been running away from God, is a fugitive out in the Sinai desert. He had settled down to a life of relative security with his wife and father-in-law and had even become a shepherd. But that's when God chose an unusual way to get his attention. Moses saw a bush on fire, but on closer perusal discovered that it wasn't being consumed. And out from the bush came a voice!

Moses never doubted God Himself was talking to him. Unfortunately, though, God was asking him to do the last thing in the world he wanted to consider. But the call was clear: "So now, go. I am sending you to Pharaoh to bring my people the Israelites out of Egypt" (Exod. 3:10).

For a man who had fled Egypt because he had killed one of Pharaoh's soldiers, this was a dubious honor, being singled out by God for "mission impossible."

Thus we hear a humorous dialogue with God at the burning bush, in which Moses recites all the good reasons for not obeying God with total commitment.

First, Moses questions his own ability. "Who am I, that I should go to Pharaoh and bring the Israelites out of Egypt?" (3:11). "Why me? There are other people, much better qualified to do the job. I'm not really qualified. I have other things I must do before I can consider this." Sound familiar? But God's reply was, "I will be with you" (3:12).

Moses counters by raising a theological question. In essence he asks, "Who are you?" To respond in obedience would involve great risk. Moses wants to be sure that this God is for real. To tackle "mission impossible" requires the utmost confidence that God is exactly who He says he is. And of all times—God's word to Moses was mysterious! "I am who I am" (3:14). This phrase defies translation. Some scholars suggest "I will be what I will be." It may be a phrase that has a similar sound to the Hebrew word for *Lord*. At any rate, it remains an affirmation that God is greater than all human understanding.

After some more excuses, Moses tries to opt out for personal reasons. He returns to where he started, "O Lord, I have never been eloquent, . . . I am slow of speech and tongue" (4:10). It's likely that Moses is reminding God he was a stutterer. This ought to settle the matter. But God isn't through with Moses. He isn't taking excuses. "Who gave man his mouth? . . . Is it not I, the Lord? Now go; I will help you speak and will teach you what to say" (4:11). At this point, I can still hear echoes of my dad's order: "Get off the dime!"

Finally Moses plays his last card: "O Lord, please send someone else to do it" (4:13). And although God shows His anger with Moses at this point, He offers to provide a companion for the task. Moses' brother Aaron, an eloquent man, is already on the way to meet Moses with ability to match Moses' commitment!

Haven't we all, from time to time, heard that voice within us calling us to some new area of venture for God? Haven't you had that "hunch" to move out into some new direction of Christian service or witness? For most of us, it won't be something great by human standards. It will probably be something quite unspectacular. But there are all kinds of acts of loving and caring that are an integral part of God's call.

7

EVANGELISM

The late Daniel T. Niles, an evangelist from Ceylon, described evangelism and witness as "one beggar telling another beggar where he found bread." To us for whom Christ has become the Bread of Life, sharing the good news with our fellow beggars will bring as much joy as when we found it for ourselves.

The next day John was there again with two of his disciples. When he saw Jesus passing by, he said, "Look, the Lamb of God!"

When the two disciples heard him say this, they followed Jesus. Turning around, Jesus saw them following and asked, "What do you want?"

They said, "Rabbi" (which means Teacher), "where are you staying?"

"Come," he replied, "and you will see."

So they went and saw where he was staying, and spent that day with him. It was about the tenth hour.

Andrew, Simon Peter's brother, was one of the two who heard what John had said and who had followed Jesus. The first thing Andrew did was to find his brother Simon and tell him, "We have found the Messiah" (that is, the Christ).

Then he brought Simon to Jesus, who looked at him and said, "You are Simon son of John. You will be called Cephas" (which, when translated, is Peter).

The next day Jesus decided to leave for Galilee. Finding Philip, he said to him, "Follow me."

Philip, like Andrew and Peter, was from the town of Bethsaida. Philip found Nathanael and told him, "We have found the one Moses wrote about in the Law, and about whom the prophets also wrote— Jesus of Nazareth, the son of Joseph."

"Nazareth! Can anything good come from there?" Nathanael asked.

"Come and see," said Philip.

When Jesus saw Nathanael approaching, he said of him, "Here is a true Israelite, in whom there is nothing false."

"How do you know me?" Nathanael asked.

Jesus answered, "I saw you while you were still under the fig tree before Philip called you."

Then Nathanael declared, "Rabbi, you are the Son of God; you are the King of Israel."

Jesus said, "You believe because I told you I saw you under the fig tree. You shall see greater things than that." He then added, "I tell you the truth, you shall see heaven open, and the angels of God ascending and descending on the Son of Man."

(John 1:35–51)

After his vivid description of John the Baptizer, John begins his Gospel with the story of five men whose lives were profoundly impacted by Jesus Himself. At the conclusion, John reflected upon his purpose in writing: "Jesus did many other miraculous signs in the presence of his disciples, which are not recorded in this book. But these are written that you may believe that Jesus is the Christ, the Son of God, and that by believing you may have life in his name" (John 20:30–31).

Without apology, John makes it clear that he writes for one reason: to witness to Jesus Christ through what He did and said, in order to bring men and women into a lifegiving relationship with Him. Thus, the entire Gospel of John was written as an evangelistic tract, and our understanding of evangelism must be shaped by John's method and style.

We must not minimize the fact that John begins with the story of five men whose lives were changed by a personal encounter with Jesus. First, there were two disciples of John the Baptizer, Andrew and one unnamed man. Then there was Simon, followed by Philip and Nathanael.

Andrew and the unnamed disciple conclude that Jesus is indeed the Christ, the Hebrew Messiah, on the basis of the witness of John the Baptizer: "Look, the Lamb of God, who takes away the sin of the world!"

It is generally assumed that the unnamed disciple is John the apostle, for John never names himself in this Gospel. Later, he refers to himself as "the disciple whom Jesus loved." Presumably, John and Andrew seek out Jesus and are invited into His house for fellowship. The fact that John specifies the exact hour suggests his personal recollection.

John tells us something very special about Andrew. After being with Jesus, the first thing Andrew did was to find his brother and bring him to Jesus. Andrew appears on two subsequent occasions in John's Gospel, each time bringing someone to Jesus. During a tense moment, in the midst of a crowd of tired and hungry people, it was Andrew who brought the boy with his little lunch to Jesus. Later, it was Andrew who brought a group of inquiring Greeks to Jesus. Andrew knew the joy of bringing people to Jesus.

Philip models the same pattern. His call was a direct invitation from Jesus Himself: "Come, follow me." Responding to that invitation, Philip, like the others, came to the conclusion that Jesus was the Messiah, God's long–awaited and hoped–for "Anointed One." And Philip's first desire was to bring his good friend Nathanael to Jesus.

Since Nathanael does not appear again in the Gospel, we're not certain of his identity, although many scholars identify him with Bartholomew by linking the two names. Nathanael Bartholomew must have lived the rest of his life with deep gratitude to Philip for introducing him to Jesus, as must have Simon Peter for his brother Andrew. Certainly, Andrew and Philip represent the first two evangelists in the New Testament.

And What Is Evangelism?

As time goes by, I find myself wishing we could declare a moratorium on some of our theological vocabulary. One of the words I would love to eliminate is "evangelism." You see, each time we add "ism" to the end of a word, we change its meaning.

In the deepest sense, "evangelism" is not a major New Testament word. "Evangel" is. The Evangel is the Good News of Jesus. It is the Good News of the abundant life that He brings, the Good News of the forgiveness of sins that causes healing and wholeness. But what happens when we add the "ism" to The Evangel? We start developing techniques and methodologies.

What is the first thing that comes to mind when you hear the word "evangelism"? I'm sure some of you think of Billy Graham preaching to thousands of people in a large stadium and on television. I have great love and respect for Dr. Graham. He has refined a particular method of evangelizing, of sharing the good news of Jesus. Nevertheless, we must not limit our understanding of evangelism to mass meetings with highly polished techniques of communicating.

To others, the word "evangelism" might conjure up a picture of an aggressive encounter by someone armed with a repertoire of Bible verses and tracts, pressing you to an acceptance of Christ lest you die before the conversation ends. All too frequently, such an "evangelist" shows little concern for you as a person and for any burdens you might be bearing. You feel more like a target for a spiritual conquest.

And some of you are tired of us preachers laying a trip on you, making you feel guilty for not being more aggressive in your witnessing to others of Christ.

If we take Andrew and Philip seriously, we need not think of techniques or methodology when we think of witness and evangelism. They simply invited a brother and a friend to come and see. There was no set method, no argumentation, no theological discussion, no outlines, no program. Just an invitation to meet a special Friend.

Evangelism Is Not an Argument

As pastor for twenty-two years in an all-too-typical suburban congregation, I'm painfully aware of our "evangelistic" ineffectiveness. The thought of "witnessing" is both foreign and repugnant to most of our folks.

I'm convinced that the myth of "the good Christian" is at the root of our problem. If we assume that people who believe in God, and to some degree in Christ, folks who live lives that are basically respectable, are "good Christians," we have consigned ourselves to a basic paralysis when it comes to "witnessing." We tend to assume that it really doesn't matter what you believe as long as you are sincere.

Yet at the same time, we are rightly repelled by a type of witnessing more characterized by the Mormon missionary or Jehovah's Witness visitors who knock at our doors with annoying regularity. And leave with predictable reluctance. Theirs is the witness of proof and argumentation. Such argument abounds in outlines and selected passages of the Bible to force the issue, presumably to the point of gaining a convert.

You would be hard pressed to find this approach in the New Testament, especially here with Andrew and Philip. The whole idea of evangelism as that of winning an argument is preposterous! If I win the argument, does the other person lose? Can anyone become a disciple of Jesus by losing an argument? I don't think so! The issue of winning and losing arguments has little, if anything, to do with evangelism.

At a dinner party the other evening I met some of the other guests for the first time. It became clear early in our conversation that many of these folks were fascinated with the fact that here was a real live, honest-to-God, clergy person.

It was obvious that these people didn't often visit with preachers, and they seemed surprised I was both interested in and conversant with many things other than religion itself. But somewhere in the course of the conversation, it was quite natural to talk about God and life in relationship to Him. Not because I'm a professional preacher and a trained theologian, but simply because Christ is central to my way of living and thinking.

The conversation had quite naturally turned to values. And how could I talk about values without reference to the One who has shaped my values? At one point, a person became argumentative, and I could only reply, "I have no desire to argue or debate, and if sharing my deepest feelings with you has offended you, I ask your forgiveness." I meant that sincerely! For to me, the winning of arguments has nothing to do with witnessing or evangelism. I prefer the style of Andrew and Philip that invites people to "come and see."

In this way, evangelism is not a matter of results. The issue is not the outcome. I'm afraid all too many of us are strangely silent when it comes to making our witness because we are afraid of rejection or defeat. Sharing what is important to us never need be a matter of argument, much less a question of winning or losing!

The Ultimate Question

Somehow, we must address the discomforting reality that most of our churches are ineffective in evangelizing the people outside their doors. This is true even in some growing churches in which the growth consists mostly of folks coming from other churches. And this ineffectiveness is due to the fact that most of us tend to be incoherent and even speechless when confronted with human unbelief.

I'm not sure whether non-evangelizing people produce non-evangelizing churches or non-evangelizing churches have produced non-evangelizing people. Either way, it is urgent that we break out of this crippling cycle. But as long as we are content to regard our churches primarily as places where we gather for worship and fellowship, and support some mission projects in other communities at home and abroad, we breed ingrown ineffectiveness.

What is really at stake is the extent to which Jesus

is central to our living and being. Too often, we try to avoid this issue by developing programs which, in reality, transfer the responsibility to someone else. Programs of mass evangelism and of visitation evangelism are too often substitutes for the kind of evangelism indigenous to the New Testament. Instead of witnessing to our own faith in Christ, we count on the professional evangelist or the person especially trained in visitation evangelism to do the job for us. We too readily support others to do the evangelizing while we continue in our own incoherence regarding the faith.

I'm convinced that we can break the impasse, not by training a few isolated folks to be evangelists, but by recovering the New Testament view of witnessing. Instead of looking for quick fixes in programs of evangelism, we really need to engage in the long, and perhaps painful, process of becoming different Christians and distinct churches.

This process will require a recovery of biblical preaching in our pulpits. This preaching must go beyond moralizing and bringing comfort to the already comfortable. It must declare the life, death, and resurrection of Jesus for the forgiveness of sins as central and normative.

The process will further require calling people to discipleship to Christ rather than to become patrons of the church. Only when people become participants rather than spectators is there any hope for the future of our non-evangelizing churches. We must not be participants in programs, but in the life in Christ.

Every time we regard evangelism as a program, we resort to programs, outlines, and arguments. But if we see it as a flow of life from one person to another, our focus will be upon maturing in Christ.

Evangelism was neither a program nor a problem in the New Testament, was it? Neither Andrew nor Philip had any hesitancy or methodology. Instead, theirs was a contagious and irresistible overflow of faith, life, and joy in the Savior. Immersed and caught up in the Spirit of Christ, their words and actions represented a continuing invitation for others to come and see Jesus.

Witnessing and evangelism, then, must become much more than programs or words designed to bring people to faith in Christ. Genuine witness will flow through our conversations and our actions in relationships as we take people seriously as belonging to God with us. Witness may flow as well through our silence when we are genuinely trying to understand the needs, fears, and aspirations of our acquaintances. Religious language is often excess baggage that erects barriers between us and other persons.

The late Daniel T. Niles, an evangelist from Ceylon, described evangelism and witness as "one beggar telling another beggar where he found bread." To us for whom Christ has become the Bread of Life, sharing the good news with our fellow beggars will bring as much joy as when we found it for ourselves. Just ask Andrew and Philip!

8

STEWARDSHIP

If our stewardship is a matter of deciding how much of our money to share with God, we will never be good stewards. But if we begin with the belief that we are managing God's money, we will experience the joy of being good stewards.

WOULDN'T YOU KNOW a pastor couldn't write a book on the Christian faith without talking about money? That's right! But not because I'm trying to get money from you! Nor am I trying to raise money for some worthy cause. I must write about money, not because I'm a fundraiser but because I'm a pastor. There's a difference? Sure!

My motive is very much in step with Jesus. For if the Gospels give a balanced presentation of His teaching, He taught more about wealth and property than about any other subject, including prayer. And yet He never had a budget to raise or a payroll to meet. He never took anything other than meals or hospitality. Why, then, did He mention money and possessions so often? Because He genuinely cared about people.

For more than thirty-five years, I've been a pastor in affluent, suburban congregations. Believe me, I've learned more than a little about what wealth does to people. All too many times I've witnessed the overwhelming power that property and possessions can wield over people. So I'm more convinced than ever that Jesus placed great emphasis upon our relationship to money and possessions because He knew human nature so completely. He also saw the potential wealth has to corrupt and destroy people.

Is money evil? Not at all. Sometimes Paul is misquoted at this point. Many times I've heard people who thought they were quoting the Bible say, "Money is the root of all evil." Not so! Money itself is neither good nor evil; it is morally neutral. It is the *use* of money that is either good or evil. What Paul really said was, "The love of money is a root of all kinds of evil" (1 Tim. 6:10).

This love of money is called greed. And greed unchecked becomes all-consuming. Recently, I preached a sermon entitled "How Much Is Enough?" I pointed out that greed is never satisfied. The apostle Paul checks greed by saying, "But if we have food and clothing, we will be content with that" (1 Tim. 6:8). Until we are able to draw a boundary that says, "This is all I need," we will be driven by greed for more and more without end.

The love of money is not the only root of evil. Evil confronts us on many fronts, and to regard money as the only or even the major root of evil may be naïve. But to those of us who have access to wealth, there is the reality of this source of evil ever present. The issue, then, is not how much money we make or control. The issue is what we do with the money at our disposal.

I think of many wealthy people I've known across the years. For some, wealth has been a great source of satisfaction. To others, it has been a source of brokenness, tension, and destruction. C. Davis Weyerhaeuser was born into wealth and multiplied that wealth through his own business acumen. I serve on two boards of Christian organizations with Dave and have become aware of the scope of his generous giving. I've also come to know something of his lifestyle—and I can tell you that he won't be featured on the television series, "Lifestyles of the Rich and Famous."

Long ago this man made a choice to be a faithful steward of whatever God entrusted to him. Instead of spending millions on lavish entertainment, travel, and luxury, he has contributed enormously to numerous Christian ministries and institutions, and these contributions have enriched the lives of countless people around the world.

Choice. It's the bottom line of stewardship, a conscious choice to regard one's wealth not as a personal possession but as a trust from God to be used for the work of His Kingdom.

What Is a Steward?

Like other Christian words, *stewardship* is not a word that we use in everyday parlance. In recent years, the closest most of us came to the word was when we were welcomed aboard the airplane by a stewardess. But since the trend to egalitarianism brought males into the ranks, instead of stewards and stewardesses, we now have flight attendants. And the word "steward" is even further removed from our working vocabulary.

To a church member of the New Testament period, though, *steward* was a much-used word describing a familiar function. In their language, the word that we translate "steward" was *oikonomos,* from which we get our word "economy."

And who was an *oikonomos?* Remember that the economy of that time was based on slavery. People were either "free" or "slave." Free people purchased and traded slaves. Slaves were the absolute property of their owners, and the owners were quite free to do as they wished with their slaves.

While Jesus never organized a program to abolish the institution of slavery, He certainly planted the seed which ultimately would lead to the abolition of it. In the history of slavery in the United States, both slave owners and abolitionists used the Bible to defend their cause. We must be careful, therefore, not to use the Bible wrongly by forcing its cultural patterns upon any given situation. Although the people of the New Testament did not take on the injustices of the economic order in the slavery of that time, the clear implications of the gospel would eventually lead to such a result.

Remember Paul's delightful little letter to Philemon? A runaway slave named Onesimus had come to Christ through the apostle's ministry in Rome. Paul requires Onesimus to return to his master, Philemon, who is a friend of Paul's and a brother in Christ. Knowing full well that runaway slaves were not treated well by former masters, Paul wrote the letter asking Philemon to treat Onesimus "no longer as a slave, but better than a slave, as a dear brother. He is very dear to me but even dearer to you, both as a man and as a brother in the Lord" (Philem. 16). It can only be a matter of time until such a system will be untenable in the light of such a high view of men and women in Christ.

But in the early days of church history, it was natural for Christians to think of themselves in relationship to Christ as they would think of the relationship of slaves to an owner. While this approach may be repugnant to us because of the attitude we have toward slavery, we must nevertheless appreciate the metaphor through their eyes.

To see oneself as a slave was not necessarily demeaning; many masters treated their slaves with dignity. It's likely that many of these Christians were slaves. In Christ, they discovered their true worth was not a matter of being slave or free, but of being loved by God.

Free and slave, they found themselves together as slaves to God. You see, slaves knew they had no rights; they had no power; they had no standing apart from their master. Happy were the slaves whose masters took them seriously and who gave them rights and privileges! Such slaves lived with a singleness of purpose—to please their master.

Thus to be regarded as a slave of Christ was not seen as a stigma but as a high calling. To be loved and wanted by the greatest and most caring of all masters was, after all, a source of great joy. This was why Paul, born a free man and a Roman citizen, consistently referred to himself as being a slave of Jesus Christ. We translate the word into "servant" in most of our translations because of our repudiation of slavery. But we do well to remember that the word used by Paul was actually *doulos*—the word for "slave."

Without compromising our opposition to any system that puts some people in bondage to other people, we must never think of Christ as anything but absolute Master and ourselves as His slaves. Our only true dignity is a gift from Him. Our worth is given to us by Him. Our standing with God is a precious gift conferred by Him.

In this light, we sense the dramatic impact of Christ's words in that upper room on the evening before His death: "I no longer call you servants (*doulous*), because a servant does not know his master's business. Instead, I have called you friends (*philous*), for everything I have learned from my Father I have made known to you" (John 15:15). While Christ calls us friends, we do well, with Paul, to remember that we are still His slaves. He will always be the Master who loves and cares for us.

Within larger households, the master found it necessary to entrust many matters of management to a competent and faithful slave. This slave was called the *oikonomous,* translated by us as "steward." The steward was thus a slave who had the responsibility of managing the household. This task included accountability for financial accounts, a position of great trust.

Christ's parable of the talents (Matt. 25:14–30) is based upon this concept of the steward. Each slave was given the responsibility for the management of a part of the master's assets until he returned. Each would have known what the master expected—a reasonable return on the principal. The underlying point of the parable is that the sum of money given to each of the stewards belonged to the master, not to the steward himself. The absolute sovereignty of the master is never questioned in the parable.

And this is where our concepts of stewardship can sometimes get out of kilter with Scripture. We want to place ourselves in some kind of partnership with God. Having been raised in a democratic and free society (thank God!), it's hard for us to relate to this metaphor of slaves and masters. But to think and live biblically requires us to fit ourselves in anyway! God is not "the man upstairs," nor my "co-pilot," nor my "senior partner." He is Lord and Master, the sovereign God and King!

We are called and trusted by this King to be *oikonomous,* faithful stewards to whom He entrusts the management of His household until He comes.

How Do We Regard Money?

Once we begin to catch the idea of the New Testament meaning of stewardship, we see two entirely different ways of viewing money and property. The normal way of viewing wealth and possessions is shaped by our culture. If we had been raised in a tribal culture in East Africa, we would view personal wealth and possessions as belonging basically to our tribe or clan. But in our tribe of capitalistic free enterprise, we have been taught that our wealth is a private possession. As a matter of fact, we hold the right to money and private property at the level of a "sacred" and inalienable right.

I'm not here to argue the respective merits of any particular economic system, but I must point out that our way of thinking about private property and wealth is not grounded in the biblical concept of stewardship. When you start with the idea that what you earn and own is your very own, even though you may give some recognition that it comes to you as a gift from God, you can't very well arrive at a concept of stewardship like that in the Bible. For when you start with the premise that your money belongs to you, you can only decide how much of *your* wealth you will give to God.

The Bible confronts us with a radically different way of thinking about wealth and possessions. Here, the perspective is grounded on the assumption that everything belongs to God and to no one else. All money, all property, all our time, all our gifts and energies—everything we are and have belongs to God. We don't own anything. We are merely stewards who are given God's trust to manage the household.

The implications of this biblical view are awesome.

We cannot start by calculating how much of our money, or time, or talent we will give to God. Just the inverse is true. We must calculate how much of the resources given to us to manage should be directed to our own interests in the light of others' needs!

The bottom line, then, is not how much we give, but how much we keep. Few of us have much to cheer about in the realm of stewardship! Most of us end up giving what we can afford and still be comfortable. And we'll keep doing this as long as we assume that what we have is ours.

The father of the Methodist church, John Wesley, was a steward who realized that everything belonged to God. He determined to hold his lifestyle to the same basic level that he had maintained as a student. As his earnings increased, he held the line on expenditures in order to make everything else available to God and others. True, Wesley didn't have to battle inflation, but he kept his personal expenses at the same level year after year. And his giving greatly increased.

A modern Wesley was Robert G. LeTourneau, an American industrialist and manufacturer of heavy earth-moving equipment. From his simple beginnings, LeTourneau became a man of great wealth. Because he regarded everything as belonging to God, he began with the biblical principle of the tithe—giving one-tenth of everything he earned to God's work. As his wealth multiplied, he increased the proportion by following Wesley's pattern. He chose to live at pretty much the same level in his wealthy years as he had in his less affluent years. After his death, it was learned that in his mature years he had chosen to live on the ten percent and to give away the ninety percent!

Do you see the difference? If our stewardship is a matter of deciding how much of *our* money to share with God, we will never be good stewards. But if we begin with the belief that we are managing *God's* money, we will experience the joy of being good stewards.

Principles of Stewardship

Once you have a handle on the ownership of wealth and possessions, you're ready to enter into a whole new world of discipleship and stewardship, a way of genuine discovery and joy.

The Bible doesn't lay a lot of rules and guilt-producing formulas on us, but ever calls us to new freedoms and joy. Imagine finding freedom from bondage to financial worry! I'm here to tell you that you *can*—but not by making more money. There are a growing number of people on television these days with all kinds of schemes for getting rich and finding financial independence. Well, I've seen more than a few folks get rich (though not in those ways), and I've seen them get more and more tangled and confused with their wealth. Bigger houses, better cars, second homes, club memberships, international travel, boats, planes, clothing. They may not look like albatrosses at first glance, but they have a heavy habit of weighing down our lives.

The only way to true freedom is the way of Christian stewardship. And it has nothing to do with accumulation and consumption. If you really want to be free, a good place to begin is to read 2 Corinthians 8 and 9.

You won't find a set of rules, but you will find principles to live by. As Paul wrote to the folks in Corinth, the believers in Jerusalem were having tough times. Poverty and famine, coupled with persecution because of their faith, had made them destitute. Other churches throughout Asia Minor and Greece quickly responded to their needs with financial offerings, much the same as we do today for hungry people in Africa or earthquake victims in Mexico.

Paul had been instrumental in making these needs known and in raising the money for relief. In writing to the folks in Corinth, who were relatively well off, he left us with some significant principles as applicable today as they were then.

To Paul, the most important thing was that "they gave themselves first to the Lord and then to us in keeping with God's will" (2 Cor. 8:5). Here is where real giving begins, or it becomes just another obligation. We have no right to ask for money first. The issue is personal commitment to Christ as Lord. There is no reason for anyone who has not first given himself to Christ to give money to the church. One of the dangers of institutional Christianity is that financial support of the church or "the cause" is too easily substituted for personal commitment to Christ.

Jesus calls us to be disciples, not patrons. There will

be many disciples who are unable to contribute to a particular cause at a given time. But we should never confuse the call to financial support with the call to discipleship.

The second principle in these chapters is that "each man should give what he has decided in his heart to give, not reluctantly or under compulsion, for God loves a cheerful giver" (2 Cor. 9:7). No one should give out of a begrudging sense of guilt or obligation. The last phrase of Paul's sentence could be translated literally, "God loves those who give with hilarity."

Giving can be an experience of joy. Sacrificial giving—giving in which we really forego some legitimate need or desire—can become fun! But only when we really believe that everything belongs to God, not to us.

For most of us, hilarious giving does not come naturally or easily. It hasn't for me. I came into the adult life scratching and clawing. I was raised in a family that was always financially marginal, to say the least. Giving away a whopping chunk of my income was not my idea of a fun night on the town! But I can say with all honesty that we have come to find some of our deepest joys in consciously reducing our consumption in order to give to others. And when we have gone without what we had every right to regard as legitimate, we have found even greater joy in knowing that we have pleased the Master.

The third principle of stewardship is quite democratic. It is the principle of proportion. "Now finish the work . . . according to your means. For if the willingness is there, the gift is acceptable according to what one has, not according to what he does not have" (2 Cor. 8:11–12).

Certainly, the tithe (ten percent) of one's increase is the basic proportion set forth in the Bible. My counsel to every young couple starting a Christian marriage is to begin with a minimum of the tithe as their basic financial commitment. In this way, we are reminded with every paycheck that the money is not ours, but God's.

For most of us, the tithe should be just the beginning of our stewardship. We may not make the ninety percent of LeTourneau, but most of us could certainly spend less on ourselves in order to be better stewards. To be sure, there are certain seasons in our lives. In recent years, we've had two or more children in colleges and universities. I consider their education a part of our stewardship, and I refuse to allow a formula to be the measure of our stewardship. But we've never found any justification for retreating to less than the tithe—and most of the time, we find great joy in doing considerably more.

As I said, there's no way this pastor can talk about the Christian faith without talking about money. How you relate to wealth and possessions will determine the very climate of the seasons of your life.

STUDY GUIDE

Chapter 1. Sin

1. What is your earliest recollection of the word or idea of sin?

2. Do you feel that people are basically good with the potential for evil or basically evil with the potential for good?

3. Can you identify sin in your life which is either hurting you or someone else? To whom, if anyone other than God, must it be confessed?

4. What steps must you take to change such behaviors or patterns?

5. Can you honestly accept God's forgiveness? Can you honestly forgive yourself? And others?

Chapter 2. Salvation

1. What does "being saved" mean to you personally?

2. How would you describe to someone unfamiliar with Christian thought what it means to be "lost"?

3. Are there any things or behaviors from which you still need to be saved?

4. How do you perceive the cross of Christ in relationship to salvation?

Chapter 3. Born Again

1. How would you have answered the young man asking you, "Are you born again?"

2. If you answered in the affirmative, recall the process or event which you perceive to have been basic to your experience of the new birth.

3. If you answered in the negative, are you satisfied with that answer?

4. How do you or could you know whether or not you have been born again?

Chapter 4. Conversion

1. Describe your own journey with relationship to Christ and conversion.

2. Are you in the process of conversion, or do you feel that your conversion is a past experience?

3. Are there changes in your lifestyle, values, and behavior that you would still like to experience?

4. How do you think God can work for change in your life?

Chapter 5. Sanctification

1. What does the word "holy" bring to your mind?

2. Can you identify with the frustration of Pastor Fleming and of Paul? How would you describe it in your own words?

3. Are there some areas of growth in your life that give you encouragement?

4. At what points are you discouraged in your spiritual journey?

Chapter 6.   Commitment

1. Do you consider yourself to be a giver or a taker? Or both? How do some significant others perceive you?

2. Are there some issues or causes in which you feel you should become involved but haven't? What has kept you from such involvement?

3. What specific steps would you have to take to venture into a new area of risk?

Chapter 7.   Evangelism

1. What is the first thing that comes into your mind when you hear the word "evangelist" or "evangelism"?

2. Which appeals most to you: evangelism as sharing good news, or evangelism as winning converts?

3. How do these differ?

4. How do you respond to the statement: "What you do speaks so loudly, I can't hear what you say"?

Chapter 8.   Stewardship

1. To what extent do you feel that your attitudes toward money and possessions shape your relationships and behaviors?

2. Do you agree that everything you have really belongs to God? If so, how do you see yourself as a steward of what is His? Rate your stewardship on a scale of 1 to 10.

3. How do you regard the idea of tithing?

4. What specific changes in your lifestyle would be required in order to direct more of your resources to the work and service of God?